Distinguished Wisdom Presents . . .

GAIN 20/20 VISION FOR THE NEW DECADE!

A STEP BY STEP PATH TO A MORE SUCCESSFUL FUTURE

Pastor Terrance Levise Turner, MBA

Well Spoken Inc.| Nashville, TN

© 2020 Terrance Levise Turner

All rights reserved. No part of this publication may be reproduced, scanned, transmitted or distributed in any printed or electronic or mechanical forms or methods, including photocopying, recording, or other without prior written permission of the publisher, except in the case of brief select quotations embodied in critical reviews and certain other noncommercial uses permitted by copyright law. For permission requests, write to the publisher, addressed below.

Unless otherwise indicated, all Scripture quotations are taken from the King James Version of the Bible.
Well Spoken Inc.
P.O. Box 291806 Nashville, TN. 37229
WellSpokenInc@bellsouth.net
www.TerranceTurnerLivingProverbs.com

Ordering Information
Quantity sales. Special discounts are available on quantity purchases by corporations, associations, and others. For details, contact the "Special Sales Department" at the address above.
Cover design by Susan of LSDdesign/99Designs.com
Book design by Terrance Levise Turner
Printed in the United States of America
ISBN 9781734482003 and 9781734482027 Paperback
ISBN 9781734482010 and 9781734482034 Hardcover
ISBN 9781734482041 Ebook

Table of Contents

Preface viii
  Part One
  Regaining Clear Vision

Chapter One The Right Perspective 1

  CHAPTER TWO A Clearer Perspective 16

Part Two

Five Essential Keys To A More Successful New Decade

CHAPTER THREE God: The 1st Essential Key To A More Successful New Decade 31

Chapter Four Marriage & Family: The 2nd Essential Key To A More Successful New Decade 58

Chapter Five Health: The 3rd Essential Key To A More Successful New Decade 98

Chapter Six Finance: The 4th Essential Key To A More Successful New Decade 115

Chapter Seven Peace of Mind: The 3rd Essential Key To A More Successful New Decade 176

  Final Words 218
    ABOUT THE AUTHOR 221

This book is dedicated to the future of people everywhere who desire a brighter tomorrow. The purpose is to give you God's perspective for living a successful life until the return of Jesus Christ.

Also by Pastor Terrance Levise Turner, MBA:

Distinguished Wisdom Presents... Living Proverbs–Volume 1

Distinguished Wisdom Presents... Living Proverbs–Volume 2

Distinguished Wisdom Presents... Living Proverbs–Volume 3

Distinguished Wisdom Presents... Living Proverbs–Volume 4

Distinguished Wisdom Presents... Living Proverbs–Volume 5

Distinguished Wisdom Presents... The Dynamic Victory Confession: Powerful Confessions For A Victorious Life!

The Earth Is Sad, Little Timmy

Distinguished Wisdom Presents... Your Wealth Is In Your Anointing: Discover Keys To Releasing Your Potential.

Preface

The writing of this book "Gain 20/20 Vision For The New Decade! A Step By Step Path To A More Successful Future" has been a journey that has required great vision and focus in the midst of changing times and perilous, unprecedented events in society. We have faced one of the worst pandemics in contemporary history. Any plans for progress or advancement by almost every business and industry has been either stalled or totally derailed. Families and individuals have experienced isolation on a worldwide scale. We were *"all in this together"* while at the same time having been forced to be separate from one another. The only way to survive such devastating circumstances is to keep a vision of a future that you refuse to let go of. Vision is the key to hope. The purpose of this book is to show you how to obtain, maintain, and fulfill a clear, godly vision for your future. You will learn how to operate in God's principles and gain stability even in disruptive times. Enjoy this book and allow it to refresh your soul and restore clarity to your perspective of God's love for you and His purpose for your life. Step by step you will achieve lasting happiness, peace, and a life well lived. You will gain a clear path to a more successful new decade and beyond!

Part One

Regaining Clear Vision

I counsel thee to buy of me gold tried in the fire, that thou mayest be rich; and white raiment, that thou mayest be clothed, and that the shame of thy nakedness do not appear, and anoint thine eyes with eyesalve, that thou mayest see. As many as I love, I rebuke and chasten; be zealous therefore, and repent.

-Revelation 3:18-19

Chapter One

The Right Perspective

As I start this book, I want to give you a story in Mark 8:22-38 that illustrates the need for clear vision. As believers in the Lord Jesus Christ, we must have clear vision in order to fulfill the Great Commission that He has given us. I want to help you "Gain 20/20 Vision For The New Decade! A Step By Step Path To A More Successful Future."

We as believers don't see things in the same way as those of the natural world. We don't see things on Earth in the same way that those outside of the Kingdom of God see it. We have hope in the world that they don't have. We are in the world, but not of the world. Our eyes have been opened. Yet, because we are in the world, we are often touched by the influences of the world. The mainstream media, social media, etc., can influence how we see the world. If we don't take time to renew our mind, then, we can need corrected vision. We can be like someone who doesn't have clear vision. We can be "farsighted". Where, all we see is going to Heaven. We can't see the "here and now" with clarity and decisiveness. All we see is escaping to Heaven. All you can see is far, but you can't see near. You may be "too heavenly minded to be of any earthly good." You can't see how you can make it from day-to-day. You can't see how you can make it next week. You can't see how you can make it through another week on your job. You can't see how you can take care of your family, or your bills. You can't see how you can get along with your husband or wife, or your children. You can't see close up. You can't see what's right in front of you and how to deal with day-to-day living. All you can see is far, but you can't see near. So, you're far-sighted. So, your hope is just for Heaven. Your hope is for getting out of here. You're "too heavenly minded for much earthly good". So, you're not focused on "occupying until He comes" (Luke 19:12-13). However, that's what Jesus said. Jesus said "Occupy until I come" (Luke 19:12-13). In other words, "take dominion". The word "occupy," means to take "dominion". When you occupy a land, then, you take possession or dominion in a land. You need to take dominion in your life. You need to take dominion over your finances, take dominion over your health, take dominion over your family, take dominion over your job, take dominion in society, take dominion in your business, etc. In other words, you need to be fit for living today. You're not just so focused on Heaven that you don't focus on today. The person who only focuses on going to Heaven, while neglecting to take dominion in their life on Earth, would be considered "far-sighted." They would need corrected vision in order to successfully prosper and thrive in today's world. God doesn't want you to just "float around" in otherworldly behavior and thinking, so as to be "too heavenly minded to be of any earthly good".

Then, contrarily, there are some people who are "near-sighted". They can see right up-close, but they can't see far. So, all they are concerned with is the cares of life. They are only consumed by what's right in front of them. They don't have a "vision" for the future. They don't have a vision for long-term prosperity, or long-term health, or long-term success. They don't have a vision for "life and life more abundantly". They don't have a long-term vision, because they are encumbered with the cares of life today. All they see is their problems.

Jesus talked about the four kinds of ground. He talked about the "sower" sowing the seed of the Word of God into the ground of people's heart.

And some seed fell by the "way side". These are the people who were not even paying attention in life. The good Word of God that had the answers for their life was all around them. It was being projected and cast in front of them and it just fell by the way side, and they didn't even allow it to enter into their hearts. They didn't even pay attention. They didn't even reach out to get it. So, the demons, or as the Bible calls them, the "birds of the air", came and devoured the Word before they could even grab hold to it. Then, there was the "stony ground". The Word was also coming to them, and it did fall on that ground, but the ground was hard. They were "hard hearted". So, they hadn't conditioned their heart to be receptive to the Word. So, when the Sun came, it scorched the Word, so that it couldn't put down roots, because they were hard-hearted. This is the "stony ground". Then, Jesus talked about those that were the "thorny ground". The "thorny ground" received the Word. It did go in, but there were "other things entering in", such as other thoughts, other concerns, other endeavors, and those things choked the Word. The Word had the power to change their life. It did take root. It started to grow, but all of the other things were vying for their attention as well. All they could see was what was right in front of them. They were "near-sighted". The other things blocked the effectiveness of the Word of God in their life.

For example, if you took your finger and put it right in front of your eye and looked up at the Moon, then, as small as your finger is compared to the Moon, your finger could block your view of the Moon. Your finger could block your view of the Moon, because of your "near-sighted" perspective. Though your finger is so small compared to the Moon, yet, it could still block the gigantic Moon, because you can't see around or through your finger if it's right up close in your line of sight. You wouldn't be able to see the glorious Moon. You wouldn't see the majesty of the Moon and the light that it brings even in the darkness. So, those that are "thorny ground" have all of these things that are encumbering their minds and their thinking. These things are right in their face and it "chokes the Word" so that it can't bring forth any fruit to completion in their lives.

Thankfully, then, there's the "good ground". Those are hearers that heard the Word and understood the Word and with patience brought forth fruit. They heard the Word. They understood the Word. And, with patience, they brought forth fruit. These people allowed the Word into their heart, it took root, and it corrected their vision for their life. So, they had hope for today and hope for tomorrow. Their vision was corrected. I want to help you "GAIN 20/20 VISION FOR THE NEW DECADE! A Step By Step Path To A More Successful Future."

Opening The Eyes of The Blind

Now let's look at Mark 8:22-38.

> 22. And he cometh to Bethsaida; and they bring a blind man unto him, and besought him to touch him.
>
> 23. And he took the blind man by the hand, and led him out of the town; and when he had spit on his eyes, and put his hands upon him, he asked him if he saw aught,

Now, notice that, they brought the blind man to Jesus, because Jesus is the answer. Jesus is the answer. He is the Healer. But, notice what Jesus did to bring healing to the blind man, or, in other words to help him "Gain 20/20 Vision" or corrected vision. He took him out of his environment where he was just surrounded by the problem or his condition. All that the people of his community knew him as was the "blind man". His entire surroundings and manner of living was as the "blind man". He was known as the "blind man" with a pan or cup in his hands and sitting on the side of the road saying, "Alms, alms, alms for the blind! Alms, alms, alms for the blind!" So, in the city that he was living in, that's all that he was known as. He was known as the "blind man". Therefore, his environment helped to amplify his condition. There were "church people" around him, and there were other ministers around that were teaching the Law of Moses, yet, the "blind man" hadn't received the true help or healing that he needed. Thus, Jesus knew that he needed to be changed from the inadequate environment of his affliction. Likewise, as a believer in the Lord Jesus Christ, you have to allow your mind to be removed from the environment of the world. The ungodly world is inadequate to meet your spiritual, mental, physical, social, or financial needs. You have to allow your mind to leave from being constantly surrounded by the problems of the world, or the perspective of the world. You must change your perspective from looking at the conditions of the world in the same way that those who are only bound to the natural world sees it. You must see the world as it really is. You must see yourself as you really are. You must see God as He is. You must see your future as God says it can be. You must not allow your mind to be impressed by the images of the world through social media, television, the music of the world, the news media, the magazines, etc. If you constantly allow the world's images to impress your mind, then, you will start to see yourself like those who do not have God in their heart. You will start to view life as being absent of the hope, power, and influence of God. You will become distorted in your perspective of God. You will see God as having less power or influence than the world system. You will begin to see Him as being incapable of solving the problems of the world or the issues of your life.

It's like the illustration, which I gave earlier, of the finger in front of your eye that can block the Moon. If you look at the finger from the wrong perspective, then, it could block the large, glorious Moon. A lot of times, that's the way that we may see the problems of the world. We may see the conditions and situations in the world or our own lives as being large and looming. Thus, we need corrected vision. Therefore, Romans 12: 1-2 says,

> 1. I beseech you therefore, brethren, by the mercies of God, that ye present your bodies a living sacrifice, ho-

ly, acceptable unto God, which is your reasonable service.

2. And be not conformed to this world: but be ye transformed by the renewing of your mind, that ye may prove what is that good, and acceptable, and perfect, will of God.

God wants you to have perfect vision. God wants you to have 20/20 vision. God's "good, acceptable, and perfect will" is 20/20 vision for you as a believer. God wants you to "Gain 20/20 Vision".

As a saint of God, you're in the world, but you're not of the world. You may wonder why the previous years didn't go as you wanted. Maybe, you lost vision. Maybe you lost clarity concerning what God has for you. So, I want to help you "Gain 20/20 Vision For The New Decade" by helping you to understand who you are as a believer. I will help you understand Who God is. This book will help you to understand what your purpose is on Earth. God wants you to have hope for today and hope for tomorrow. God doesn't want you to be shaped into the image of the world, but He wants you to be transformed by the renewing of your mind through His Word. This is how you will be able to see clearly for the new decade. He wants you to see that you are a victor and not a victim, above only and not beneath, the head and not the tail, and, the winner and not the loser. You gain corrected vision by spending time meditating God's Word. Corrected vision comes from hearing God's Word. Corrected vision comes from looking at your life through the lens of God's Word and gaining a revelation for your life. Corrected vision comes by allowing your vision to be adjusted through the revealing power of the Bible. God's "good, acceptable, and perfect will" is 20/20 vision for you.

In 3 John 2, God says, "Beloved, I wish above all things, that you may prosper, and be in health, even as your soul prospers." In other words, "God wishes above all things that you prosper, and be in good health, even as you allow your mind, will, emotions, personality, disposition, intellect, to prosper or to be adjusted to God's perfect vision for you." This is how you "Gain 20/20 Vision For The New Decade!"

Environment Impacts Perspective

Now, let's look back at Mark 8:22-38.

> 22. And he cometh to Bethsaida; and they bring a blind man unto him, and besought him to touch him.
>
> 23. And he took the blind man by the hand, and led him out of the town; and when he had spit on his eyes, and put his hands upon him, he asked him if he saw aught.

Jesus led the blind man out of his normal environment of blindness. His normal environment was continually re-emphasizing to him his condition of blindness.

> 24. And he looked up, and said, I see men as trees, walking.

So, the blind man didn't have the right perspective of other men. He didn't have the right perspective of those surrounding him. He saw his problem as large and looming. He saw others as large and looming over him like "trees." He had the wrong perspective of himself. He had low self-esteem. Otherwise, why would he see "men as trees" (large, tall, and looming), and he saw himself, (who was also a man) as small, insignificant, and powerless. He saw others as large, tall, and looming like trees. He said, "I see men as trees, walking." He didn't have 20/20 vision. He didn't have perfect vision, due to his condition of blindness and due to the environment that he was living in. And, that's one of the reasons why Jesus took him out of the town. In the town, his low self-esteem and condition was continually being amplified and reinforced in his mind. The message that he was continually hearing was "You're the blind man. You're the blind beggar on the side of the road. You're helpless. You're not enough. You're insecure. You're vulnerable." That's how he felt. He felt the ever-present, depressing, disempowering feeling of being the "blind man." God doesn't want you to feel that way during this new decade. He wants you to be hopeful. God wants you to be empowered with proper vision for your life and future. God wants you to know Who He is. God wants you to know who you are. God wants you to have hope in Him for today and the future. He wants you to have faith for today, so that you can see "near", and, He wants you to have hope for tomorrow, so that you can see "far". God wants you to have 20/20 vision. Mark 8:25 says,

25. After that he put his hands again upon his eyes, and made him look up: and he was restored, and saw every man clearly.

He made him "look up". He made him "look up" to the Source. He made him look up to God. You see, when you can see God clearly, then, you can see yourself clearly. He made him "look up!" God wants you also to be able to look up. He doesn't want you to just be looking at the world. He doesn't want you to just look at what's surrounding you. He doesn't want you to just look at the problems. He doesn't want you to be conformed to this world, but, He wants you to be transformed by the renewing of your mind, so that you may prove what is that good, and acceptable, and perfect will of God (Romans 12:1-2). God wants you to have perfect "20/20 Vision For The New Decade". Jesus told the blind man to "look up", and when he looked up he was "restored". The scripture didn't just say his eyes were opened. It didn't just say his eyes were healed. Rather, the scripture said that, "he was restored". He was restored spirit, soul, body, socially, and financially. He was restored to his proper status in life. He was restored in his family life. He was restored in his health. He was restored in his finances. He was restored in his peace of mind. He was restored in his self-esteem. He was restored in his relationship with God, because he could look up. He could see God clearly. He could see himself clearly. He could see others clearly. And, he could see his future clearly. Mark 8:25 says,

> 25. After that he put his hands again upon his eyes, and made him look up: and he was restored, and saw every man clearly.
>
> 26. And he sent him away to his house saying, Neither go into the town, nor tell it to any that are in the town.

In other words, "Now that you have been made whole, and now that you've been restored, don't go back to the way you used to live. Get rid of your beggar's garments. Put away your beggar's cup. You're no longer the "blind man". You need a new attitude, because you've been made into a new person. You've been "restored". You're looking up and you know who you are now. You can go forward into your best life. The rest of your life can be the best of your life. Don't let yourself be shaped, and pressed, and conformed into the person that they say you used to be. Don't even go back there. Don't even go back to the condition that you used to live in. Don't even think back to where you used to be. I want you to "GAIN 20/20 VISION FOR THE NEW DECADE!" so that you can see clearly. I want you to see life as it is. I want you to see that you're blessed today and you have hope for tomorrow. Because, you've looked up!"

What Jesus did for the formerly "blind man" was an illustration for you, because He wants you to see Him clearly. He wants you to look at Him, because when the blind man looked up "he was restored and he saw every man clearly." Jesus wants you to look up. He wants you to look up to the risen Savior. He wants you to look up, so that you will know that you have hope in this world. He wants you to know that "you're in the world, but not of the world" (John 17:14). He wants you to know that you have victory through Jesus. He wants you to look up to know Who He is, and, thus, who you are. Thus, you have hope in the world. That's how you "GAIN 20/20 VISION FOR THE NEW DECADE

Chapter Two

A Clearer Perspective

Jesus's disciples were with Him when He healed the formerly blind man. Jesus was going to use the healing of the formerly blind man as an illustration to them. Now, He's going to bring it on home to them. Jesus continues in Mark 8:27,

> 27. And Jesus went out, and his disciples, into the towns of Caesarea Phillipi: and by the way he asked his disciples, saying unto them, Whom do men say that I am?

In other words, Jesus was asking them "How do others see me? Based on what you've heard? Do others have the proper vision of me?" You remember that the formerly blind man "looked up: and he was restored, and saw every man clearly." He looked up to Jesus and he was "restored, and saw every man clearly." But, now Jesus is talking to His disciples and He asked them the question "Whom do men say that I am?" He's asking them "How do others see me, based on what you've heard?"

> 28. And they answered, John the Baptist: but some say, Elias; and others, One of the prophets.

In asking them "Who do others say that I am?" Jesus was leading up to the question "Who do you say that I am?" In other words, "Do you see me clearly?" "You've been walking with me for this period of time. You've seen me do the miracles. You've heard my Words. Yet, Do you see me clearly?"

> 29. And he saith unto them, But whom say ye that I am? And Peter answereth and saith unto him, Thou art the Christ.

So, Peter had clear vision. He had a clear revelation. Vision is revelation. That's the subject of this book. I want you to "GAIN 20/20 VISION FOR THE NEW DECADE!" Vision is revelation. Vision is when something is revealed unto you.

For example, if I take off my glasses, then, things are not clear to me. I can see shapes. I can see the images to a certain degree, but it's not as clear as it could be. However, when I put my glasses back on, then, the details of the images becomes clear. The details of what's in the room or the writing, etc.; becomes more clear.

So, Peter had a revelation. He said, "Thou art the Christ." But, Jesus wanted to give them "20/20 Vision" so that they could see the full details. The purpose of this book is to give you the full details and the path to a more successful future.

> 30. And he charged them that they should tell no man of him.
>
> 31. And he began to teach them, that the Son of man must suffer many things, and be rejected of the scribes,

and be killed, and after three days rise again.

So, Jesus began to teach them in order to "adjust" their vision. He was teaching them in order to bring further revelation to them. Jesus was beginning to refine their vision so that He could get them to the point of 20/20 vision regarding their future.

It was like going to the eye doctor. He or she will have you look through a lens. The eye doctor will then make adjustments back and forth with the various strengths of lenses to see which one helps you see the clearest. He or she will ask you "Do you see better this way or that way?" Or, he or she may ask, "Is number one clearer or number two?" And, according to your responses, he or she will know how close you are to obtaining 20/20 vision and which prescription to write for your glasses or contact lenses. The goal is to get you to 20/20 vision with the adjustments. You're getting corrections for your vision so that you can have 20/20 vision when you walk out of the eye doctor's office. According to your responses during the exam, the eye doctor will know how clear your vision is. So, God wants you to "Gain 20/20 Vision For The New Decade!"

When Jesus healed the formerly blind man, He touched him and asked him the question "If he saw aught?" Or, in other words, "Do you see anything?" The man responded "I see men as trees walking." So, Jesus knew that He needed to make another adjustment to his vision. So, He touched him again. And, the man "looked up." He gained the proper perspective by "looking up." The Bible says, " . . . And he was restored, and saw every man clearly." That's what God wants for you. He wants you to "GAIN 20/20 VISION FOR THE NEW DECADE!" As you go forward this year and into the new decade. No matter what your previous year was like. No matter what the previous 10 years were like. No matter "the good, the bad, or the ugly", God wants you to see clearly as you go forward into the new decade. He wants you to have hope for today and hope for tomorrow. There's hope for today, in spite of the problems, and in spite of the issues. There's hope for next week on your job. There's hope for next week in school. There's hope for you raising your children. There's hope for your relationship with your husband or wife. There's hope for you. And, God wants you to know that there's hope for the future. There's hope for the next 10 years. There's hope for the next 20 years. There's hope for the next 30 years. There's hope for the next 40 years. There's hope for the next 50 years, should the Lord tarry. And, if He does return before then, then you have the eternal hope of Heaven. He wants you to keep your eyes on the long-term as well as the near.

> 31. And he began to teach them, that the Son of man must suffer many things, and be rejected of the elders, and of the chief priests, and scribes, and be killed, and after three days rise again.

So, Jesus was teaching them so that they could see clearly why He was here. He wanted them to see that "This is not just about us walking around from city to city and healing people and multiplying fish and loaves and me walking on the water." He said, "No. I have a purpose for being here." Jesus was bringing them into clarity of vision, because they were coming into a critical time in His ministry. They were also coming into a critical time in their life and new ministry. They were coming into a critical time in their life regarding their future. The amount of clarity that they had regarding the significance of the next few weeks would determine how effective they would be after Jesus was crucified, buried, resurrected, and ascended back to

Heaven. Their clarity would determine how they would make it through the reality of His crucifixion. It would also empower their passion to carry out the Great Commission, which is why they had walked with Him over the last three and half years. They had to see clearly why He called them and choose them to be His disciples.

This is the primary key needed for you to "GAIN 20/20 VISION FOR THE NEW DECADE!" Not only is it about God blessing you financially. Not only is it about you making it through your daily life on your job, school, and daily living, etc. Rather, you have to know that you have a "Great Commission." You have a purpose. It's about souls being saved. It's about spreading the Gospel of Jesus Christ. Everyday that you're in the world you have to be aware that you're not "of the world." It's not about just hanging out on social media, or watching television, or just relaxing. No. You're on a mission. You need to "GAIN 20/20 VISION FOR THE NEW DECADE!" by living on purpose. You need to live with passion. You need to live with focus. You must know that you're living for a specific reason. God saved you on purpose. God saved you with a purpose. He changed you for a purpose. He taught you for a purpose. He delivered you for a purpose. He demonstrated His glory and grace to you for a purpose. God wants you to "GAIN 20/20 VISION

FOR THE NEW DECADE!" God says, "This is critical to your future as a believer". This is critical for the changes that are coming into society. There are changes coming over the next year, two years, three years, five years, etc. He wants you to be ready for them. He wants you to have hope, but He also wants you to be prepared. He wants you to see clearly. When you see clearly, then, you can see what's on the horizon. You can see the sunshine, but you can also see the storm on the horizon. You can see the dark clouds on the rise. You can see the opportunity and you can see the opposition. You can see clearly when you have "20/20 Vision". You can navigate accordingly. Mark 8:31 continues,

> 31. And he began to teach them, that the Son of man must suffer many things, and be rejected of the elders, and of the chief priests, and scribes, and be killed, and after three days rise again.
>
> 32. And he spake that saying openly. And Peter took him, and began to rebuke him.

So, Peter had a moment of revelation when he said, "Thou art the Christ." He could see clearly that Jesus was the "Christ." Yet, he couldn't see beyond himself and the other disciples traveling from town to town with Jesus, as Jesus healed and demonstrated His power. He thought Jesus was going to use that power to overthrow the Roman government and bring in a glorious kingdom that would put Israel into a position of power. However, Peter didn't see the Roman cross that Jesus would be crucified on in order to deliver all people from the bondage and penalty of sin. He didn't want to see the test. He didn't want to see the pain. He didn't want to see the pain that came before the gain. He didn't want to see the pain that came before the glory. His eyes were obscured from seeing the pain of the cross that Jesus had to hang on in order to deliver all of us from the penalty of sin. Yet, that was the central purpose for Jesus coming to Earth in a human body. Without Him going to the cross, then, all else would have been for naught. So, Jesus was causing them to "GAIN 20/20 VISION" regarding themselves and why they were here. He was teaching them Who He was, and what their future held. He wanted them to gain a passion for their purpose. When you can see clearly, then, vision provokes passion. That passion comes from purpose. When you can clearly see your purpose, then, you can develop a passion to pursue it. So,

Jesus was helping them to "GAIN 20/20 VISION." Just as Jesus healed and corrected the vision of the formerly "blind man", He was also correcting the vision of His disciples regarding their true purpose. This was essential, because they would be the carriers of His Gospel after He was resurrected and ascended back to Heaven.

Seeing Clearly For The Road Ahead

So, Jesus was still teaching. Even when correcting Peter. He didn't necessarily turn and look at Peter to bring the correction. Rather, He used Peter as a teaching moment. Jesus used Peter's out-spoken response and inability to clearly see His purpose as a teaching moment to all of His disciples. He allowed this to be a teaching moment for further correction of the vision for all of His disciples. Mark 8:32 continues,

> 32. And he spake that saying openly. And Peter took him, and began to rebuke him.
>
> 33. But when he had turned about and looked on his disciples, he rebuked Peter, saying, Get thee behind me, Sa-

> tan: for thou savourest not the things that be of God, but the things that be of men.

The purpose of the vision correction was because Jesus didn't want His disciples to "savor" or over-value the things of men more than they valued the things of God. As a born-again believer, you must not "savor" the things of men more than the things of God. Whether it's your job, in your family, in your community, etc., or whatever you are involved with. You have to savor the things of God more than you savor the things of mankind. As you interact with society, you must remember that you're in the world, but you're not of the world. You are an "ambassador" for Christ. You are an emissary in a foreign land. You are a pilgrim traveling through the world. Therefore, you must remember that you're on assignment. You're assigned to the "Great Commission." Thus, you must know that you are a "chosen generation, a called out people, a royal priesthood" (1 Peter 2:9). You must realize that you have an assignment. When you see yourself clearly in this way, then, you won't allow the problems of the world to pull your heart down. You won't allow the problems of the world to bring your spirit down. The reason that you have hope is because you are like the formerly "blind man." You have "looked up" and your eyes are upon Jesus, and you know your Redeemer lives! And, He's holding you up in this world. You also know that your ultimate inheritance is not in this Earth, but your inheritance is on High. So, you have hope for today, because "if God be for you, then, who can be against you?" And, you have hope for tomorrow, because you have Heaven as your eternal home. You can see near and far. You have "20/20 Vision". Mark 8:34 continues,

> 34. And when he had called the people unto him with his disciples also, he said unto them, Whosoever will come after me, let him deny himself, and take up his cross, and follow me.
>
> 35. For whosoever will save his life shall lose it; but whosoever shall lose his life for my sake and the gospel's, the same shall save it.
>
> 36. For what shall it profit a man, if he shall gain the whole world, and lose his own soul?
>
> 37. Or what shall a man give in exchange for his soul?

38. Whosoever therefore shall be ashamed of me and of my words in this adulterous and sinful generation; of him also shall the Son of man be ashamed, when he cometh in the glory of his Father with the holy angels.

God wants you to "GAIN 20/20 VISION FOR THE NEW DECADE!" He wants you to know who you are as a child of God. He wants you to know Who He is as your Lord and Savior. He wants you to be fully cognizant that Jesus is the head of your life. He wants you to know why you are here. You are the "light of the world." You are the "salt of the earth." However, "if the salt has lost its flavor or savor (or purpose or vision of why it's here or its effectiveness), then, "it is good for nothing, but to be cast out and trodden under foot of men." That possibly may be a reason for some of the trials that you went through in the prior decade. God wants you to be effective and flavorful for the new decade. Therefore, in this first half of this book, He is correcting your vision regarding the "Great Commission". He wants you to have a vision for today and for eternity. He wants you to be all that He called you to be. He wants you to have "life and life more abundantly" (According John 10:10). He wants to be able to get the highest use out of your life on Earth. He also wants you to live fully cognizant of your eternal purpose. You're here on purpose. He wants you to live with passion. He wants you to clearly "Gain 20/20 Vision For The New Decade! A Step By Step Path To A More Successful Future."

Part Two

Five Essential Keys To A More Successful New Decade

I. God

II. Marriage & Family

III. Health

IV. Finances

V. Peace of Mind

> Where there is no vision, the people perish: but he that keepeth the law, happy is he.
>
> -Proverbs 29:18

Chapter Three

God: The 1st Essential Key To A More Successful New Decade

In Proverbs 2:1–11, the Bible tells us how through seeking to obtain the wisdom of God, we can enhance and increase our relationship with Him.

1. My son, if thou wilt receive my words, and hide my commandments with thee;

2. So that thou incline thine ear unto wisdom, and apply thine heart to understanding;

3. Yea, if thou criest after knowledge, and liftest up thy voice for understanding;

4. If thou seekest her as silver, and searchest for her as for hid treasures;

5. Then shall thou understand the fear of the Lord, and find the knowledge of God.

6. For the Lord gives wisdom: out of his mouth comes knowledge and understanding.

7. He lays up sound wisdom for the righteous: he is a buckler to them that walk uprightly.

8. He keeps the paths of judgment, and preserves the way of his saints.

9. Then shall thou understand righteousness, and judgment, and equity; yes, every good path.

10. When wisdom enters into thine heart, and knowledge is pleasant unto thy soul;

11. Discretion shall preserve thee, understanding shall keep thee.

As we receive the Word of God from the Bible, we will increase in our relationship with God. If we learn to incline our ears to wisdom, and actively apply our heart to understanding God's Word, then, we will increase in wisdom, and as we increase in wisdom, then, we will also increase in our relationship with God. God is the source of wisdom. You must actively seek wisdom and you must recognize when wisdom is being presented. You must incline your ears in the direction of wisdom when you find it. You must be someone who has an appetite for wisdom. You must be someone who has an appetite for the advantage in life. Wisdom gives you the advantage in life. Wisdom gives you the edge in life! Wisdom gives you the "inside scoop" on life. Wisdom is the "open door for more" in life. Wisdom is the answer for "how-to." Wisdom shows you "how-to-do-it", "how-to-get-it", "how-to-be-it", and "how-to-take possession" of all that is good in life. Wisdom is the edge. Therefore, when wisdom is going forth, you should want to be the kind of person who has loved God in such a way and sought God's Word in such a way that you have developed an appetite for wisdom. You can sense when something is the wisdom of God for your life. So, wherever wisdom is coming from you have developed an appetite for wisdom so much so that you incline your ear toward wisdom. There used to be a commercial on television that said, "When E.F. Hutton speaks everybody listens." It showed people walking down the street and when E.F. Hutton spoke everybody would *lean over* in his direction to hear what he had to say. They inclined their ear to listen when E.F. Hutton spoke, because, they knew that as a financial advisor, he had the inside scoop. He had the inside scoop concerning financial advice. Or, someone may have, what people calls, "the Midas touch." It's where whatever they buy, then, everybody else wants to buy it. Or, whatever they invest in, then, everybody wants to invest in it, because, they have "the Midas touch." In other words, everything they touch "turns to gold." Or, you may want to find out what a person who is very successful is investing in? You may ask: "What stocks are they investing in?" Everybody wants to find out. So, they incline their ear when that person opens their mouth. Warren Buffett has an annual meeting where he talks about his company, Berkshire Hathaway, and people want to gather in on that meeting and hear his presentation. Why? It's because, he has been the wealthiest person in the world for multiple years. Therefore, people want to know "What is Warren Buffett investing in?" They want to know "What does Warren Buffett say about the economy?" They ask: "What does Warren Buffett say about this or that?" They incline their ears toward his wisdom. Well, even more, you should incline your ear to God's wisdom about your life. God knows what you should invest in. God knows what relationship you should invest in. You may be a young person in a relationship or you may be considering a new relationship? You should acknowledge God about that relationship. God knows who your husband should be. God knows who your wife should be. You may be considering starting a new career? God knows what job you should be taking. God knows what school or college you should attend. God knows what neighborhood you should live in. God knows all things regarding your life. And, so, you have to be ready to incline your heart toward His wisdom. So, if you learn to incline your ears to wisdom and actively apply your heart to understanding God's Word, then, you will increase in wisdom. As you increase in wisdom, then, you will also increase in your relationship with God. God is the source of all godly wisdom. So, the number one key to help you "Gain 20/20 Vision For The New Decade" is for you to have a personal relationship with God. Having a strong relationship of reverence with God is the first source of wisdom. The Bible says, "The fear of the Lord is the beginning of wisdom" (Proverbs 9:10). In other words, the reverence of God is the beginning of wisdom.

God reveals Himself to us through the Bible

God reveals Himself to us through the Bible. The Bible is the written Word of God. It is the only source that we have of God's thoughts and commandments to humanity. That's the importance of the Bible. In the Book of Acts it says of Jesus: "There is none other name under heaven given among men whereby we must be saved"(Acts 4:12). That's the importance of calling on Jesus. You won't get born-again by calling on other names or religions, no matter the religion. You can call on various religious figures, but you will not receive eternal life. You can have certain disciplines and religious practices, such as dietary rules and lifestyle rules, and you can have a more disciplined life, but you won't go from death to life through other religions. Only by Jesus are you born again. It's evident by millions and millions of lives that have called on Jesus. He is a "whosoever will God." The Bible says in John 3:16, "For God so loved the world . . ." So, God doesn't discriminate. He doesn't say, "You have to be from this nationality", "Or, this group of people." No. He says, "For God so loved the world, that he gave his only begotten Son, that whosoever believeth in him should not perish, but have everlasting life." John 3:17 continues, "For God sent not his Son into the world to condemn the world, but that the world through Him might be saved." The Bible says, "There is none other name under heaven given among men whereby we must be saved"(Acts 4:12). That is the importance of our relationship with God. This is the key to gaining clear vision for your future on the earth and into eternity. The Bible has been proven by millions of people to be true and reliable. Living by God's principles brings health and life. God is life. God is love. God is righteousness. God's ways are *just* right. You don't have to be highly religious. You just have to be highly rational to follow God's ways and principles. You just have to be someone who wants to have a good outcome in life. You can say, "Well, I want a good outcome in my health, in my family, in my marriage, in my finances, and I want to know where I'm going to go when I die . . . And, I heard that the Bible has answers to a good life on this earth for my family, finances, my health, and eternal life in Heaven with God, my gracious Creator, when this life is over. Well, it's just rational that I pursue these principles." It's not by works, but it's by faith. So, faith is action. Faith is not a feeling. You may just make a rational decision. You may say, "You mean God promises eternal life? Well, I know that I didn't make myself, and He says, when I close my eyes for the last time, then, I could go to Heaven simply by accepting Jesus as my Lord and Savior? The Bible says, 'There is none other name under heaven given among men whereby we must be saved'

(Acts 4:12)? The Bible says, His principles promises good health and peace with God, peace with myself, and peace with others? I want peaceful relationships and good health . . ." Well, when you recognize that exercising God's principles brings quality of life in this world and eternal life when this world is over, then, that really takes a load off! Having that truth and assurance really takes a load off while walking through this world. Nowadays, there are people living unto 100 years of age or older. With the current healthcare and nutrition that we have available to us and lifestyle amenities to help enhance our life, then, it is very reasonable to believe that you could live to close to 100 years of age. Wouldn't it be wonderful to go through your life without that question mark over your head of "Where am I going to go when I finally die?" And, wouldn't it be wonderful to go through life with principles that are enhancing your life, enhancing your health, enhancing your relationships, and enhancing your finances? Wouldn't it be wonderful to go through life with that load off by simply casting your care upon the Lord, the Creator of Heaven and Earth? You didn't create the Sun. You didn't create the stars, or the Moon, the planets, the seas, the trees, and you didn't create yourself? Yet, wouldn't it be wonderful to put your faith in the One that the Bible declares did create those things? Wouldn't it be wonderful to call upon the

Lord and test Him and see? The Bible tells you "O taste and see that the Lord is good" (Psalm 34:8). So, He gives you an opportunity to try Him out. You may be someone who wasn't raised up in the Church and with Christian values. Yet, you may have heard that "Jesus saves and delivers and gives life and life more abundantly." Then, the Bible says, "O, taste and see that the Lord is good" (Psalm 34:8). So, you can "taste and see", and as you go along and realize that . . . "Hum . . . this is turning out pretty good." Why? Because, everybody has trials and everybody has situations and circumstances. Yet, the Bible says in Psalm 34:8, "O, taste and see that the Lord is good. Blessed is the man that trusteth in Him." God is so wonderful by giving you the opportunity to "taste and see." It's like God is standing there in the "Grocery Store Aisle of Life", and He has little sample cups of His goodness, and as you pass through the aisle of life, He says, "Would you like to try some?" He says, "Taste it and see." And, you reach over and taste a little bit of His goodness by praying and saying, "Lord, help me. Help me with this situation with my family. Lord, help me. I'm trying to figure out life. Lord, help me. I'm trying to figure out where to go for college. Lord, help me. I don't know anything about God. I don't know too much about God. But, Jesus, if you're there, please help me. Hear me." You're "tasting" to "see", and He will prove Himself to you. He will say, "I'm here." And, He will start to open doors for you. Then, He says, "The full package is 'On-Sale' right now for free! Right there on aisle 'Salvation!' I've already 'paid it in full' for you! It's right over there. All you have to do is reach out and take it by faith! It's right there on aisle 'John 3:16!' The Bible says, 'For God so loved the world, that He gave His only begotten Son, that whosoever believeth on Him should not perish, but have everlasting life. For God sent not His Son into the world to condemn the world, but that the world through Him might be saved' (John 3:16-17). Yes! You can get saved today! 'Taste and see that the Lord is good!' Amen!" God is good. His ways are good. He loves you. He wants you to "prosper, be in good health, even as your soul prospers" (3 John 2). The Bible is the only reliable, proven source from which we gain successful living from obeying God's instruction to people. The Christian hymn says, "Jesus paid it all. All to Him I owe. Sin was like a crimson stain, but He washed me white as snow." The scripture says, "For by grace are you saved through faith; and that not of yourselves: it is the gift of God: Not of works, lest any man should boast" (Ephesians 2:8-9). The way you get saved is simply by believing and accepting Jesus Christ as Lord and Savior by faith. Salvation doesn't come from you doing penance or smiting yourself. It's simply by believing and accepting it. The scripture says, "Whosoever calls upon the name of the Lord shall by saved" (Romans 10:13). How can you call upon Him? The Bible says, "How can they call without a preacher? And, how can he preach unless he's been sent?" (Romans 10:14) Well, I'm preaching the Word to you right now. You are hearing the Word in your heart as you read this book. The Bible says, "Whosoever calls upon the name of the Lord shall be saved" (Romans 10:13). If you've never received Jesus Christ as Lord and Savior, then, you are now hearing the Word of God. The Bible says, "So, then faith comes by hearing and hearing by the Word of God" (Romans 10:17). The Book of Romans also says, "Whosoever calls upon the name of the Lord shall be saved" (Romans 10:13). You are saved simply by asking Jesus to come into your heart. So now, if you have never received Jesus Christ as Lord and Savior, then, please simply pray this prayer:

"Jesus, I believe that you are the Son of God. I believe that you died on the cross to pay for my sins. I accept your payment for my sins. I accept you as my Lord. Thank you Jesus. I am saved. I am born-again. Amen."

Salvation is a free gift. God, your Heavenly Father, made salvation available to everyone, because He loves us so very much. It's not His will that any of spend eternity separated from Him in a place called Hell, which was not created for us. Hell was created for Satan and the demons that rebelled against God and was casted out of Heaven. They are the ones that are causing all of the "killing, stealing, and destroying" (According to John 10:10). Everyone that has obeyed God's principles for living has increased in their understanding of God, and their love for God, and their love for one another. God's principles are principles of love, peace, success, prosperity, health, and all things pertaining to the good and abundant living. One of the key principles of God is to "Love your neighbor as you love yourself." Jesus said, "Thou shalt love the Lord your God with all your heart, and with all your soul, and with all your mind. This is the first and great commandment. And, the second is like unto it, Thou shalt love thy neighbor as thyself" (Matthew 22:37-38). Those that have chosen to live their lives by God's principles have also increased in success in life. In Proverbs 2:3–4, King Solomon reveals to us how important and critical it is for us to seek God's wisdom.

3. Yea, if thou criest after knowledge, and liftest up thy voice for understanding;

4. If thou seekest her as silver, and searchest for her as for hid treasures;

The Bible Is The Only Source For Success

He says we should "cry out for wisdom!" We should "lift up our voice for understanding". I remember as a child, my mother teaching me and my brothers the Book of Proverbs in the Bible. Often, before she went to work or before we went to school, she sat down with us in our small, orange brick apartment in the housing project we lived in at the time, and prayed with us and taught us the proverb of the day. There were many dangers in the neighborhood we lived in once we went bounding out of our backdoor onto the sidewalk leading to the cement basketball court near our backyard. As we explored other parts of the neighborhood, looking to join a pick-up basketball or football game with the fella's, we had to be careful of the constant threat of danger, trouble, or temptations that could present themself at anytime, like someone wanting to fight, or someone smoking, drinking, or smoking marijuana. The principles that my mother constantly poured into us, helped to give us some kind of reference point for choosing the right thing when faced with temptations. By the grace of God, me and my brothers made it out of the limiting brick walls of the housing projects without getting caught up into smoking, drinking alcohol, drugs or babies outside of marriage.

As I became an adult, I continued to study the Book of Proverbs as a source of wisdom and guidance for life. I literally obeyed the scripture in Proverbs 2: 3 that says, "Yes, if you cry out after knowledge, and lift up your voice for understanding!" I remember one day in my cramped bedroom in my apartment as a young adult, sitting on the side of my bed. I had the Bible opened to this passage, underlined in black ink and highlighted in yellow. I looked up towards Heaven, and simply obeyed the scripture. I literally cried out to God with my voice and asked for wisdom. I asked Him to give me understanding so I could be successful in life. I said, "Father, give me wisdom! Father, give me understanding! So, I can be successful in life." I realized that I needed wisdom. I realized that I was "simple" regarding a lot of things in life. "Simple" means ignorant or naïve or not understanding or inexperienced in regard to many things in life. I was a young man, and I had not experienced many things in life. I knew I was intelligent. Yet, I also felt the enormity of the challenges that loomed over my future as I increased in age as an adult. Having lacked the advantage of a father in the home, (which could have given me and my brothers some shortcuts to learning many important things about manhood), I knew that, in many ways, I was inexperienced. I'm thankful that I did have the benefit of a faithful grandfather, who shared his time and wisdom to assist my mother in our development. However, I had the wherewithal and intelligence to go to the Source of all wisdom for what I didn't receive along the way, which is God. There are 31 chapters in the Book of Proverbs. There are typically 31 days in the month. Therefore, I continued to study a chapter of Proverbs a day, which furthered my relationship with God as my Heavenly Father.

The Bible says in Proverbs 2:4 "If you seek her as silver, and search for her as for hid treasure". This describes how valuable God's wisdom is. Wisdom starts with your relationship with God. The Bible says, "The fear of the Lord is the beginning of wisdom" (Proverbs 9:10). Everything else that you build and gain needs to be set on the foundation of your relationship with God. You should base all of your decisions on your relationship with God. You should ask, "What does God's Word say about this? What does God say about it? Is this decision right with God? Is God pleased with this choice? Would the Lord be pleased with me doing this, going here, saying this, interacting with this person, taking this job, going to this place, etc.?" It should all go back to your relationship with God. Reverence for God is the beginning of wisdom. Jesus says in Matthew 7:24-25,

> 24. Whosoever hears these sayings of mine and does them, I will liken him unto a wise man which built his house upon a rock:
>
> 25. And the floods came, and the winds blew, and beat upon that house, and it fell not; for it was founded upon a rock.

But, Jesus talked about another person that He called a "foolish man" or a "foolish person" in Matthew 7:26-27,

> 26. And every one that heareth these sayings of mine, and doeth them not, shall be likened unto a foolish man, which built his house upon the sand:

> 27. And the rain descended, and the floods came, and the winds blew, and beat upon that house; and it fell: and great was the fall of it.

There is a difference between the "wise person" and the "foolish person". The "wise" person in the parable that Jesus taught built his or her house on the "rock", which is the solid foundation of God's Word. That solid foundation comes from receiving from the Source. The solid foundation comes from a relationship with God. The solid foundation comes from entering into a relationship with God by obeying His principles. In other words, "the fear of the Lord is the beginning of wisdom" (Proverbs 9:10). Or, in other words, "the reverence of God is the beginning of wisdom". This person built his or her life upon the solid foundation of that relationship with God. He or she built his or her life upon that Rock. Jesus says that person was esteemed as a wise person. So, "when the rains came, and the winds came, and the floods came and beat upon that house, it did not fall, because it was built upon a rock." The "foolish person" was the person who heard the Word, but he or she did not do it. He or she heard about Jesus. He or she heard about the Bible. He or she heard about God, but this person did not submit to God by entering into a relationship with God by accepting Jesus as Lord and Savior. He or she did not follow after God's principles. This person heard about His principles, but they didn't want to enter into relationship with the Prince of Peace. They heard about the principles, but they didn't want to enter into relationship with the Prince. They heard about the principles, but they didn't want to submit to the Lordship of Jesus. So, Jesus said, "They built their house upon the sand." Well, what is sand? Sand is when you break up the rocks or stones into small, small, small, small pieces, then, it becomes like sand. So, that's like the principles. The principles are component pieces of the Rock, but it's not the fullness of the Rock in its solid form that you can build upon. It is component pieces. The "sand" is as if you broke up the Rock into small, small, small component pieces. However, you will be disappointed if you try to build your life only on the principles, without having relationship with the Rock, Who is the Source. When the "floods, the wind, and the rain" come, then, you will disappointed. It's because you haven't built on a solid foundation. The "floods, wind, and rain" are things such as, health problems, marriage problems, family problems, end-of-life-questions, etc. Another example is when you're faced with questions such as, "Where are you going to go when you close your eyes for the last time?" It is during such times that the Bible says, "then, that house fell". In other words, "That life fell and that person fell" Your "house" is your very life. The Bible says that the person who built only on the sand "house fell and great was the fall of it." When the Bible says, "great was the fall of it" it means utter destruction. It leads to utter destruction, which is eternal damnation in a place called Hell, which was not prepared for mankind, but for Satan and his demons. God, the loving, Heavenly Father, made provision for us to avoid hell in this life and eternal Hell. Jesus said that He is the "way, the truth, and life; no man cometh unto the Father, but by me" (John 14:6). You may have had some principles. You may have governed your life according to some success principles, which is the "sand" or component pieces of the Rock, but, if you didn't have relationship with the Rock, which is the Source, then, Jesus calls you "foolish." You wanted to hear about Him, but you didn't want to obey Him. You didn't want to enter into relationship with Him. The Bible says in Proverbs 2:4 "If thou seekest her as silver, and searchest for her as for hid treasures." A relationship with God and His wisdom is extremely important. The wisdom of God leads you into a great relationship with God. So, the principles should lead you back to the Prince of Peace. You hear certain motivational and inspirational teachers talk about the "Law of Attraction." They often use the scripture "As a man thinketh in his heart, so is he . . ." (Proverbs 23:7a). This is a true, biblical principle. However, the principles should lead you back to the Prince, which is Jesus Christ, the Creator of all things. The principles should lead you to God, the Heavenly Father, Who is the Creator of all eternal laws. The principles should lead you to relationship with the

Prince. Jesus is the Prince of Peace. He is the Source. You should build the security of your life on having relationship with Him. If you're only living your life by the principles, but you're not in relationship with Him, then, you're missing the boat. It's relationship with Him that's going to bring you into eternal life, and also make your life on Earth truly solid. Relationship with God is the source of all success in life. No matter what level of success you may attain to in your natural life, if you fail to establish a healthy relationship with God, then, you are missing the entire purpose of life. The Bible continues in Proverbs 2:5, "Then shall you understand the fear of the Lord, and find the knowledge of God". That's the most important thing. You don't want to go through this world and not know God. You don't want to go through your whole life not knowing where you're going to go when this life is over. You know the world didn't start with you and it's not going to end with you. You're just passing through. You should want to know "what's after this!" At max, you may live close to 100 years of age or a little over, but that is just a drop in the bucket in relation to eternity. Yet, the time that you live on Earth is an opportunity. Your life is a divine opportunity for you to come into relationship with your Creator. Your life is your divine opportunity to walk this planet in relationship with your Creator by walking according to His principles. But, the principles are not the relationship. The relationship comes from the person. It comes from knowing Him. Thereby, knowing Him should lead you to walk in the principles. The Bible says, "the fear of the Lord is the beginning of wisdom" (Proverbs 9:10). "The fear of the Lord" is the foundation for proper behavior in life. Reverence of God should be the guiding force behind all your decisions. To know that you have God in your heart, you have the Holy Spirit living inside of you, you have God, the Father, watching over me, you have the Lord Jesus Christ, Who died for you, and shed His blood for you, seated on the right hand side of God Almighty, making intercession for you, you have the angels of God surrounding you and encamped around about you, you live in the Kingdom of God, you live in a spiritual dimension, you are in the world, but not of the world, you're never by yourself, you're surrounded by God's presence, the Holy Spirit is living inside of you, your body is the temple of the Holy Ghost, your physical body is the "house of God", God lives inside of you, you are holy, you are set apart, you are called of God, you are sanctified, you are the temple of God for His purposes in the earth, you are a demonstration of God in the earth, God watches over you, Almighty God watches over you, you're living underneath the shadow of His wings, you abide under His feathers, you abide under the shadow of His wings, The Lord Jesus Christ is on the right hand side of God making intercession for you continually, In Him you live, and move, and have your very being, and you are God's offspring." When you know these things, then, that is true wisdom. Having eternal security is true wisdom. Because, you know that you're never alone. There's nothing anybody or any situation can do to ever truly defeat you. God is for you. He's your provider. He's your source of good health. He's your Healer. He's your Deliverer. "If God be for you, then, who can be against you?" (Romans 8:31) He's your Rock. On Him you can depend. Reverence for God should be the guiding force for all of your decisions. Reverence for God should be the guiding force for all of your thoughts, words, and actions. That's the foundation. That's the Rock. Therefore, as you establish yourself in understanding God's wisdom from the Bible, then, your relationship with God will be established and your life will become more secure. Your relationship with God is the foundational key to help you "Gain 20/20 Vision For The New Decade!" It is the foundation on your path to a more successful future. If you have never received Jesus Christ as Lord and Savior, or if your relationship with God has grown cold, due to doubt and unbelief, then, I would like to give you the opportunity to sure up the foundation for your future. The foundation for success in your future is your relationship with God. The Bible says, "Whosoever shall call upon the name of the Lord shall be saved." We are saved by grace, through our faith in the death, burial, and resurrection of the Lord Jesus Christ to pay for our sins and redeem us back into fellowship with our Heavenly Father. So, your exercise of faith is to simply ask Him to come into your heart by faith. You have heard the Word of faith through this book. So, I want you to pray this prayer right now:

"Heavenly Father, I thank you for what you've done for me through your holy Son Jesus Christ. Lord Jesus, I accept you as my Lord and Savior. I believe that you are the Son of God. I believe that you died on the cross to pay for my sins. I believe that God raised you from the dead for my salvation. I accept the salvation that you've given to me through your death, burial, and resurrection. I thank you now that I have eternal life. And, I will live for you for the rest of my life. Thank you Heavenly Father. In Jesus name, Amen."

If this is your first time praying that prayer, then, I want to say, "Welcome to the family of God". You now have the foundation for a successful future in this life and in the life to come.

Also, if you prayed that prayer in rededication to God as your Heavenly Father, then, thank God for this opportunity to bring corrective vision to your life so that you can "Gain 20/20 Vision For The New Decade! A Step By Step Path To A More Successful Future."

Now spend time building further relationship with God as your Father, by reading the Bible, prayer, and church attendance. God is your source. He is the source of salvation. That is the first point of wisdom for your life.

Chapter Four

Marriage & Family: The 2nd Essential Key To A More Successful New Decade

Proverbs 24:3–6 reveals to us the process for becoming successful in your marriage and family. This is what it says:

> 3. Through wisdom is an house built; and by understanding it is established:
>
> 4. And by knowledge shall the chambers be filled with all precious and pleasant riches.

5. A wise man is strong; yes, a man of knowledge increases strength.

6. For by wise counsel thou shalt make thy war: and in multitude of counselors there is safety.

Often, it's a real war to live a successful life in marriage and family. Why is it a war? It is because there are so many challenges. There are internal challenges, external challenges, spiritual challenges, financial challenges, health challenges, societal challenges, etc. But, the Bible reveals to us wisdom for being successful in marriage and family. In Proverbs 24: 3 the Bible says, "Through wisdom is a house built, and by understanding it is established . . . " By gaining understanding of one another in marriage and family is that house established or made stable. The Bible continues in Proverbs 24: 4 "...And by knowledge shall the chambers be filled with all precious and pleasant riches." You gain wealth and riches by gaining "knowledge." In Proverbs 24: 5, the Bible says, "A wise man is strong." It's not just someone who is *muscle bound* that is strong. Rather, the Bible says, "A wise man is strong". In Proverbs 24:5 it continues to say, "A man of knowledge increases strength." A sign that a person is wise is that they are actively seeking to increase in knowledge, and, thereby, you increase in strength, because the gaining of knowledge is the key to having power. The application of knowledge is power. The gaining of knowledge empowers you to apply that knowledge. You have to actively pursue knowledge. Proverbs 24: 5-6 says,

> 5. A wise man is strong; yes, a man of knowledge increases strength.
>
> 6. For by wise counsel thou shalt make thy war: and in multitude of counselors there is safety.

So, it is wise to get knowledge and to be a person that has a desire for knowledge. You will increase in your strength by seeking to acquire more knowledge and counsel. First of all, it's wise to develop the appetite for wisdom. Earlier in the book, I talked about the need for you to be the kind of person who inclines your ear toward wisdom. You should be someone who "Cries out for wisdom"(Proverbs 2:3). You should be someone who "seeks (wisdom) as silver, and searches for (wisdom) as for hidden treasure" (According to Proverbs 2:4). You should be someone who "inclines your (heart) toward wisdom" (According to Proverbs 2:2). You have reached a place of becoming wise once you get to that place. You will be the kind of person that will be always listening, always learning, always seeking, always looking, always inquiring of the Lord, and always inquiring of the information that He's made available. You will be more fortified in life. You will be stronger in life. You will be more successful in life. You will be more impenetrable to the forces that would oppose you in life. This is necessary for the safety and success of your marriage and family.

Plan For Success

The Bible gives us clear wisdom regarding the importance of gaining and applying knowledge for success in marriage and family. Proverbs 24: 3-4 says,

> 3. Through wisdom is an house built; and by understanding it is established:
>
> 4. And by knowledge shall the chambers be filled with all precious and pleasant riches.

It is through the gaining and applying of knowledge that you will become prosperous as a family. You obtain financial prosperity by getting knowledge. A leading family is a learning family. A learning family is a leading family. Everybody in the house should be learning. Not only should the children be in school. Rather, the parents need to be studying, reading, and learning. They should be learning how to become better parents. The husband should be learning how to become a better husband. The wife should be learning how to become a better wife. The family should be learning about budgeting and finances. Your entire family should be learning about their gifts and talents. You should be learning ways that you can make more money. Your whole family should sit down and have strategy sessions to discuss how you can come together and maximize the advantages of your family size, education, unique skills, etc. If you have two or three sons and daughters, then, you should be planning right now and discussing the question, "How can we raise our children in such a way that they can be established in a family business that they can take over when they become adults and build on their own when we get older? How can we start to educate and train them now to take over the business when they become of age?" You should start something now while they are young. Let them invest in it. Give them their allowance and then sell them some stock in the company after you incorporate it.

Sam Walton is reported to have sold stock to his children when he first started Walmart. It was in the beginning of the company before it was a multi-billion dollar company. He sold enough stock to his children so that they would have a vested interest in the company in order to maintain ownership within the family once he passed away. He allowed his children to invest in Walmart when he first started the company, in preparation for when he became older and passed away, so that, they would rightfully own the majority shares of the company. They owned it fair and square, because they bought stock while they and the company was young and small. Thereby, Sam Walton's estate avoided having to pay billions of dollars in inheritance taxes, because his children were already majority shareholders of his estate from the beginning before it became the largest and most successful multi-billion dollar retailer in the world. Now, that's wisdom! That's wisdom that should be imitated. In Proverbs 13: 20, the Bible says, "He that walketh with wise men shall be wise . . ." By reading and imitating the strategies and good sense of one of the most successful retailers and families in the business world, then, you and your family can also obtain a greater degree of success and long-term wealth. Proverbs 24: 3 says, "Through wisdom is an house built; and by understanding it is established." However, in the case of Sam Walton's founding of Walmart, he had to be wise during the early stages of founding the "house." The Bible says, "...by understanding it is established." Sam Walton and his wife, had to understand from the beginning of the company, that there would be some changes in the future. The "house" had to be established so that in the future they wouldn't lose majority ownership of the "house". Thus, the principles that you establish in your children from the beginning will make the greatest difference regarding their long-term stability. Proverbs 22:6 says, "Train up a child in the way he should go: and when he is old, he will not depart from it." Why does the Bible teach us this? It is because, your children are going to get older and you're also going to get older. They will not always be under your watch and guidance for every decision. They will grow up and go on in life in many regards. However, if you have put down an anchor of godly principles in them while they were in your house as little children in their formative years concerning right and wrong, godly principles, managing money, being respectful to parents and elders, being respectful to authority, being considerate of other people ("doing unto others as they would have done unto them") (Luke

6:31), being clean and having good hygiene, etc., then, they will live their lives according to those principles. If you instill these things in them while they are small, then, when they become older, and the boat drifts away from the shore or dock of their beginning place into the deeper places of life and maturity, then, the anchor of what they've learned will continue to hold steady. When the storms of life come and the winds blow, and the waves crash, then, they won't drift out to sea into "never-never land". Rather, the anchor of the principles that you have taught them will hold them steady in life. An example may be, when they get older and become independent college students. When they interact with other ways of thinking from other young people, then, the anchor of their morals will continue to hold. Or, when they get married to someone from a different type of family than yours, then, you want their basic morals and principles to hold steady. Why is this important? It's because everyone's family is somewhat different in how they were raised. Yet, you, as a parent, want the godly principles that you taught your children growing up to continue to hold. Therefore, if you raised your children with good, godly morals and principles, then, they can bring those values into their marriage and also pass them on to their children. Proverbs 24:3-6 says,

3. Through wisdom is an house built; and by understanding it is established:

4. And by knowledge shall the chambers be filled with all precious and pleasant riches.

5. A wise man is strong; yes, a man of knowledge increases strength.

6. For by wise counsel thou shalt make thy war: and in multitude of counselors there is safety.

This passage helps you "GAIN 20/20 VISION FOR THE NEW DECADE!" in your marriage and family. Verse 6 says, "A wise man is strong; yes, a man of knowledge increases strength." It says, "A wise man is strong . . ." He could look like "Mr. String Bean." However, if he's taking care of his family, then, the Bible says he's "strong." He has investments. He has his house in order. He has his children in order. He has prepared to send his children to college. So, it's not just the physical size of the man. No. The Bible says, "A wise man is strong; yes, a man of knowledge increases strength." A sign that you are wise is that you're continuing to pursue knowledge so that you will increase in strength. Only the wise appreciate wisdom. A sign that you are wise is that you appreciate wisdom. A sign that you're unwise is that you don't appreciate wisdom. You just appreciate your own thinking. You don't even pay attention to wisdom. You don't incline your heart toward wisdom when it comes. You're self-willed. You don't listen until life itself has to knock you on the side of your head. That's the only way that you will learn if you don't develop an appetite for wisdom. Yet, only the wise appreciate wisdom. You recognize that there are some things that you don't know. There are some things that you still need to know. Proverbs 22: 3 says, "A prudent man foreseeth the evil, and hideth himself: but the simple pass on, and are punished." Therefore, in order to have a successful marriage and family you must build your house upon the principles of God's Word. This is how you will "GAIN 20/20 VISION FOR THE NEW DECADE!" in your "Marriage and Family".

God's Word Is The Foundation For Marriage

Now, the Bible lets us know the foundation for a stable home and family. A stable family should be built upon the principles of God's Word. God's

Word is His wisdom. Therefore, a stable family should be built upon the wisdom of God. It is wise for a man and a woman to get married, and to begin to build a family. God encourages men and women to marry. Therefore, as you obey God's principal to marry, rather than to have sex outside of marriage, then, you are operating in God's wisdom. Sexual relationships outside of marriage leads to disease, broken emotions, children out of wedlock, increased poverty, and a broken society. The sexual urge is natural between a man and a woman. However, God has given us the gift of marriage as being the proper relationship for that urge, drive, and desire to be fulfilled. Healthy marriages are the foundation for a healthy society. Anything outside of God's plan for marriage is destructive to society, because it's not life giving. The Bible is the source of wisdom for marriage. As a man and a woman enters into marriage, becoming husband and wife, and learns to understand one another's differences, then, their home and family will become established. Again, Proverbs 24: 3-6 says,

> 3. Through wisdom is an house built; and by understanding it is established:

4. And by knowledge shall the chambers be filled with all precious and pleasant riches.

5. A wise man is strong; yes, a man of knowledge increases strength.

6. For by wise counsel thou shalt make thy war: and in multitude of counselors there is safety.

The Bible instructs the husband to love his wife "as Christ loves the church" (Ephesians 5:25). The Bible instructs the wife "to reverence her husband as unto the Lord" (Ephesians 5:22). The Bible instructs the children to "Honor your father and mother, that your days may be long upon the earth and it will go well with you"(Ephesians 6:1-3). As members of a home begin to understand one another's differences, and obey God's principles for family life, the home will become stable and established. So, as the husband and wife and children in that home begin to understand one another's differences, such as personality differences, etc., and as they learn how to work with one another, then, that home will become established. Not only must the husband and wife learn to understand and work with one another's differences, but the children must also be understood. The parents have to learn to work with the differences in their children. All children are not the same. Each person is an individual. A wise parent learns how to deal with their child individually. They can't let someone else tell them how to raise their child. They can receive advice concerning best practices, however, the parent should know the individual personality and needs of their child. A child really appreciates a good parent that they know is on their side. Thank God for a good parent that the child knows is on their side. If you're a child and you can say "My mother and my father are on my side. If the teachers are not on my side, or if the other adults in my family are not on my side, then, I know I have a comrade and confidant in my mother and father." That's security for a child. For a child to know that they have someone on their side and that someone understands them brings security to a child. If a child goes through their life feeling like no one understands them, then, that makes a child distraught and feel hopeless. A lot of teenagers go through that phase where they feel that nobody understands them. You must always remain the parent, but you also want to be considered as a trusted friend by your child as well. You're the parent. That's established. You're the authority. That's your ultimate position in the relationship. You know that and they should clearly discern that from the beginning. For example, as my mother was raising me and my brothers, one of things I appreciate her saying is, "You can always talk to me. You can express freely what you have on your mind and what you have questions about, as long as you're respectful in how you say it." And, that created an open door of communication. We could always have communication with our mother growing up. We could express how we felt about a situation. She was always the final authority, but we could talk about it. That's a good relationship in a family between children and their parents. Proverbs 24:4 continues,

> 4. And by knowledge shall the chambers the filled with all precious and pleasant riches".

Strive For Financial Freedom

The key to a marriage and family becoming financially wealthy and prosperous is for the husband and wife to commit to increasing in knowledge. This is an essential area for you to "GAIN 20/20 VISION FOR THE NEW DECADE: A Step By Step Path To A More Successful Future." Often, the husband and wife are just trying to get along and survive from week to week, without having a clear plan, path, and strategy for financial freedom and to build generational wealth for their family. However, financial wealth should be a critical, intense focus of your marriage and family from the very beginning of the wedding day. The focus of your marriage and family should be on increasing in knowledge. You should focus on getting the edge in life from the very beginning. You should focus on your family thriving and not just surviving in the new decade and the future decades to come. The key to thriving is learning. Learning families are leading families. Leading families are learning families. You and your family should take time out of the daily grind to read. Turn off the T.V. and read something that's going to give your family an edge. Learn about something that you can do together as a family. Discover the gifts that you have as a family. Discover your strengths as a family. Read to find out how you and your family can use your gifts and talents to get out of the daily grind. Find out how you can gain some "extra" in life, so that you can build your way to a better future. It may be that you and your family will start to study how to invest in the stock market. Or, it may be that you will start doing research on how to save money to buy and renovate houses to sell them at a profit or to use them for rental property. Maybe someone in your family is gifted in writing? So, maybe the other members of the family will study on how to help to sale and market the books. Make it a family business. Maybe someone in your family is an outstanding singer/songwriter/recording artist? So, maybe the other members of the family can get behind that person to help promote their concerts and appearances or travel with them to help work the product table or do crowd control. Thereby, everyone in the family can gain another source of income and freedom. It could be a chance for a new life for the entire family. Furthermore, maybe someone in the family is good at making pottery? So, the other members of the family will study how to market online and SEO strategy. Or, another member of the family should study how to gain mass distribution for the pottery. Or, maybe other members of the family will travel to trade shows and conventions to help make the pottery available to larger outlets. Maybe your grandmother or grandfather has a special recipe that's been passed down through the family? So, maybe a family member who has more business knowledge can study how to make this recipe or collection of recipes available in commercial quantity and quality. That recipe can become a family inheritance. The goal is to work together to come out of poverty and thereby, make it better for the entire family. Maybe you have an outstanding young person in your family who is very gifted? So, everyone in the family should get behind that child to help them advance. You make sacrifices for them to go to special schools and college. Some children or young people are naturally gifted athletically. So, everyone in the family should get behind them to make sure that they have what they need to be an outstanding athlete. The whole family should get behind whatever is an advantage or strength in that family that will help make that family successful. Therefore, Proverbs 24:4 says, "And by knowledge shall the chambers be filled with all precious and pleasant riches". The key to a marriage and family becoming financially wealthy and prosperous is for the husband and wife to commit to increasing in knowledge.

Only through increasing in practical knowledge will the home become financially free. There are some things that every home needs to know. For example, you may have a 30-year mortgage or 15-year mortgage. You must ask yourself "How can we pay this house off faster?" "Is there something that we can do to get a big influx of income?" Or, "Is there a way that we can pay more every month so that it cuts the time that we have to pay it off and cuts down the amount of interest on the loan?" That knowledge is available. There are certain strategies for this type of financial advantage that is available. Or, maybe you and your whole family should decide to do a financial success plan like Dave Ramsey's *Financial Peace University*. One of the strategies for getting out of debt is what he calls the "Getting Out Of Debt Snowball". You as the head of your household can say to your family "Family, this is what we're going to do. We're all going to do the Financial Peace University. We're going to do the 'envelope system.' We're going to do the 'Getting Out Of Debt Snowball.' We're going to pay off the smallest debt. Then, take that money that we were paying on that debt and add it to the payment on the next smallest debt. Then, take the payment amount that we were paying on the previous two smallest debts and add it to the payment of the next smallest debt. Then, take the payment amount from the previous three smallest debts and add it to the payment toward the next smallest debt. Do this until we have all the smallest debts paid off. Then, take the payment amounts that we were paying toward the small debts and add it to the lowest car payment and keep paying until you pay off your lowest car payment, so that you can have at least one debt free car. Then, take the amount that we were paying on the smaller debts plus the lowest car loan that you paid in full and add that up together to pay toward our house until we can actually pay off our house faster in fewer years. In doing so family, we can debt free!" So, everybody in the family has to be working together toward that goal. You may have to say to your children "We will get you that special gift that you want, but not right now, because we're all working toward getting our family out of debt." So, again, a husband and wife should commit to increasing in knowledge, because only through increasing in practical knowledge will the home become financially free. It is the husband's job to provide leadership regarding finances in his home according to 1 Timothy 5:8. This is what it says:

> 8. But if any provide not for his own, and specially for those of his own house, he hath denied the faith, and is worse than an infidel.

Plan For The Future

To "provide" is to have a vision for the future and to make provision or preparation for it in advance. Again, to "provide" is to have a vision for the future and to make provision or preparation for it in advance. Therefore, it is required of the husband to "GAIN 20/20 VISION FOR THE NEW DECADE!" It's the job of the husband to do what's necessary now to create provision for the future. To "provide" is to do what's necessary today to create provision for the future. That's providing. It could be the traditional providing of working a 40 or 50 hour a week job to provide daily provision, have a savings, investing, retirement fund, etc. That's traditional providing. Or, it could be working your regular job, plus starting a small business on the side that, if you work at it, it could create more income for your family in the future than your job and make the future more secure. So, again, 1 Timothy 5:8 says,

> 8. But if any provide not for his own, and specially for those of his own house, he hath denied the faith, and is worse than an infidel.

It's the husband's responsibility to provide leadership regarding finances in his home. It's his job to create provision for the future. It's his job to be doing something today and to be looking forward toward the future. The second half of the word "provide" is "vide." It is the root of the word "video." The Webster's New Dictionary defines the word "vide" like this:

Vide

1. To direct attention to a particular page in a book, etc.

2. To see before in the book, etc.

3. To see below; to see further on in the book, etc.

In other words, it's the job of the husband to be the prophet and visionary of his house and to see the rest of the story for his family. He should be seeing ahead into the future and writing the desired outcome for his family's story today.

The pronoun "pro" means "before". Therefore, to "provide" means, "to see before". It means to have a "video" in your mind of what's going to happen in the rest of the story before it happens and to make provisions to make sure that the story turns out favorably for your family. There should be a constant video going on in the mind of the husband regarding how he wants his family's story to turn out. He should be working now to make his family's life "happily ever after." He should have a vision today for the future of his immediate family, as well as his future generations. Proverbs 13:22 says,

> 22. A good man leaveth an inheritance to his children's children: and the wealth of the sinner is laid up for the just.

It's the job of a good husband to take hold of enough wealth during his life so as to be able to provide an inheritance for his children and grandchildren. He should work to take possession of the financial resources that are available in the earth, through the use of his gifts and talents, so as to gain enough wealth to deliver his future generations. That's how the "wealth of the sinner" will be transferred into the hands of the just. It will be through the "just" working practical principles of diligence, industry, and ingenuity. Husbands and wives must work together to seek God for wisdom for the financial prosperity of their family. Then, they will be able to take hold of their financial inheritance for their family. Therefore, "vide" from the word "provide" has to do with "video." It means to "see before". It means to have a vision for the future. It means to see your family is going to need more in the future and make preparations for it. The future is coming. You're getting older. You're going to need something for the children. You're going to need to pay for the children's college. Maybe, the children may need braces for their teeth. Also, at some point, a parent or spouse may need additional healthcare. Therefore, it's the job of the husband to "provide" and see ahead of time and to do something today to make sure that provision is there in the future when the family needs it. It is his job to obtain God's vision for his home and family. Through his relationship with God is where the husband gains wisdom to provide for his family. A husband's wisdom to have a vision for the future and the wherewithal to meet the needs for his family comes from his relationship with God. A part of the husband and wife's job together is to be getting the knowledge necessary to make long-term provision for their family. Again, Proverbs 24: 3-6 says,

> 3. Through wisdom is an house built; and by understanding it is established:
>
> 4. And by knowledge shall the chambers be filled with all precious and pleasant riches.

5. A wise man is strong; yes, a man of knowledge increases strength.

6. For by wise counsel thou shalt make thy war: and in multitude of counselors there is safety.

Find Out

There's nothing wrong with not knowing at first. What you don't know, you just don't know, but you need to find out. Therefore, God gives you time. He gives you resources. He gives you grace. He gives you opportunities to find out, so that you can make the most of what you have. God wants you to make the most of your time, your opportunities, your learning ability, and your intelligence, because you can always do better. You can always do better. You don't have to give up. You don't have to just accept what life gives you. You don't have to just say "Oh well, there's nothing for me. I can't do any better. Something good happens to others, but not for me. There are no opportunities for me. There are no opportunities for me and my family. We're just making it. We're just scraping the bottom of the bucket." No! You can always do better. You can always learn more. There are libraries. It's called the public library for a reason. You don't have to pay. There are free books that you can learn from. You can get a library card and check them out for free. Public school is free. They even have free lunch at school! There are no excuses. There are people who have come from the bottom and climbed their way up to the top, and so can you. Proverbs 24: 4 says,

> 4. And by knowledge shall the chambers be filled with all precious and pleasant riches.

So, it's the husband's job to obtain God's vision for his home and family. It's the wife's job to help the husband to pursue and accomplish God's vision for their home and family. It's the wife's job to be a complement to her husband. It's her job to be "help" and not a hindrance. She has to know what her assignment is in the marriage. When the wife knows what her assignment is and the husband knows what his assignment is, then, he can lead according to the vision that God gave him, and then, they can teach their children what God has said, and that household can be on one accord. Thus, that household can prosper and can be established. Genesis 2:18 says,

> 18. And the Lord God said, It is not good that the man should be alone; I will make him an help meet for him.

God made Man a "help" that was suitable for him. The wife was made to be complimentary for him. She is particularly fitted for him. Not only was she made to compliment him or fit him physically, but, she was made to help him. She was made with a fit and a function. She was made to fulfill his natural desires, and she was made with a function to help him accomplish God's purpose for his and her life on Earth. She was created to help the man fulfill the vision for his and her life together and their family. The man was already created with a vision and job to carry out. God gave him the woman as his wife to help fulfill the vision. He already had a job when God created the Garden of Eden, prior to God creating the woman to help the man. Genesis 2:5-9, 15-16, 18 says,

5. And every plant of the field before it was in the earth, and every herb of the field before it grew: for the Lord God had not caused it to rain upon the earth, and there was not a man to till the ground.

6. But there went up a mist from the earth, and watered the whole face of the ground.

7. And the Lord God formed man of the dust of the ground, and breathed into his nostrils the breath of life; and man became a living soul.

8. And the Lord God planted a garden eastward in Eden; and there he put the man whom he had formed.

9. And out of the ground made the Lord God to grow every tree that is pleasant to the sight, and good for food; the tree of life also in the midst of the garden, and the tree of knowledge of good and evil.

15. And the Lord God took the man, and put him into the garden of Eden to dress it and to keep it.

16. And the Lord God commanded the man, saying, Of every tree of the garden thou mayest freely eat.

18. And the Lord God said, It is not good that the man should be alone; I will make him an help meet for him.

So, in verse 15 God gave the provision and a job. God gave Man a vision of what He wanted him to do. He wanted him to "keep" the Garden. It is his wife's job to help her husband to pursue and obtain God's vision for their family's financial prosperity and success (Genesis 2:18). Only through gaining practical knowledge will the home be financially established. A learning family is a leading family. A leading family is a learning family.

Proverbs 24:5 says, "A wise man is strong; yes, a man of knowledge increases strength." Therefore, it is the job of the husband to increase in wisdom for the sake of establishing his home financially and in every way. The husband is the head of his home. God, the Father, is the head of Christ. Christ is the head of the husband. The husband is the head of his wife. The husband and wife is the head of their children. They have the responsibility for raising their children up in the nurture and the admonition of the Lord. The greatest sign of strength for a marriage and family is the degree of wisdom that that home is operating in. It is not the physical size of the husband, or the physical beauty of the wife that determines the strength of the home. Rather, it is the submission of that home to the wisdom and ways of God that will determine the success and financial stability of the home. Proverbs 31: 30-31 says,

> 30. Favor is deceitful, and beauty is vain: but a woman that feareth the Lord, she shall be praised.
>
> 31. Give her of the fruit of her hands; and let her own works praise her in the gates.

So, a self-sufficient, intelligent, able wife is an advantage to a husband who is submitted to God, because she is a proper help for him. They are comparable to one another in regard to fulfilling God's purpose for their life and family. Proverbs 24:6 says, "For by wise counsel thou shall make thy war: and in multitude of counselors there is safety."

Get Wise Counsel

In this portion of the book I am helping you "GAIN 20/20 VISION FOR THE NEW DECADE!" regarding "Marriage & Family". Getting "wise counsel" helps you to be equipped to win in the "war" of achieving a successful marriage and family. To win in marriage and family really takes preparation and commitment. Therefore, you should equip yourself to win in marriage. You should equip yourself with good counsel. You should talk with a couple that has had a long, successful marriage and ask for counsel for your new marriage. You should also read books written about success in marriage and family. You may not always be able to interact with certain people to get counsel in person. However, there are books that have been written about how to succeed in various areas of marriage and family. There are books that teach principles for success in raising children, success in budgeting and finances, retirement planning, etc. The knowledge is available. You should get counsel from various sources on different topics in order to give your marriage and family the equipment to be strong and fortified. The husband and the wife should be actively pursuing counsel from those who have gone before them and learned wisdom for success. Once that home is established in marriage, one of the chief goals of that family should be increasing in wisdom, knowledge, and know-how, so that that family can become financially free. God wants that family to be financially free so that the family can leave an inheritance to their children and grandchildren. Proverbs 13: 22-23 says,

> 22. A good man leaveth an inheritance to his children's children: and the wealth of the sinner is laid up for the just.
>
> 23. Much food is in the tillage of the poor: but there is that is destroyed for want of judgment.

Therefore, the husband and wife has to gain knowledge in order to become free, so that they can create enough income for their children and children's children to also be free. That's the will of God. Proverbs 19:14 says,

> 14. House and riches are the inheritance of fathers: and a prudent wife is from the Lord.

It's the will of God for you to have financial freedom. It's not God's will for you to be in debt. Proverbs 13:22-23 says,

> 22. A good man leaveth an inheritance to his children's children: and the wealth of the sinner is laid up for the just.
>
> 23. Much food is in the tillage of the poor: but there is that is destroyed for want of judgment.

This scripture says, "There is that is destroyed for want of judgment (or knowledge and understanding)". A learning family is a leading family. A leading family is a learning family. Proverbs 13: 22 says,

> 22. A good man leaveth an inheritance to his children's children: and the wealth of the sinner is laid up for the just.

The Sure Sign of Success

A sign that the husband has fulfilled his responsibility is that he has accumulated enough wealth so that he has provision to leave to his children and to his "children's children (or grandchildren)". It starts with the husband. The wife is to help the husband achieve God's vision for that household. They are to work together. The sign that they have successfully fulfilled their responsibility to their family is that they leave something tangible to their family, such as houses, property, land, businesses, investments, etc. Of course, God wants you to leave an inheritance of righteousness and moral living. However, it's the responsibility of the husband and wife to leave a tangible inheritance to their children and even to their grandchildren. This proves that you did a good job and that you taught your children. Not only did you leave enough for your children, so that they could be free and have something tangible to empower them financially, but you also left enough so that your grandchildren would also have the accumulated wealth of two generations. Your wealth and effectiveness went to the second and third generation. This will prove that you did a good job at being profitable in life. Also, it proves that you taught your children financial principles so that they could teach your grandchildren. The reason that Abraham was called "God's friend" is because God said, "I know that he will teach his children" (Genesis 18:17-19). He taught his children God's principles of tithing. Abraham "gave tithes of all" (Genesis 14:20). He taught Isaac to give tithes of all. He taught his children how to do business. He taught his children how to negotiate. He taught his children how to buy land. Abraham bought his gravesite in preparation for his death and his wife's, Sarah's, death and burial. So, his sons Isaac and Ishmael knew where to bury their father when he died. During his life he had made provision for his death and burial, because he knew death was coming. So, when his wife, Sarah, died, he already had a tomb in the land to bury her. He had a tomb in the land already prepared for his sons to bury him when he died. He already bought the property. So, he taught those principles of investing, buying property, buying cattle, and buying land to his sons. That's how the "wealth of Abraham" was transferred to the next generation. Someone had to maintain wisdom. Proverbs 13:22 says,

> 22. A good man leaveth an inheritance to his children's children: and

> the wealth of the sinner is laid up for the just.

It says, "The wealth of the sinner is laid up for the just." You often hear the saints talking about the "Great wealth transfer." The only way that the "wealth of the wicked will transferred to the hands of the righteous" is if the righteous get the wisdom that the wicked already has regarding financial accumulation and management. You have to get wisdom on how to manage money in order for God to commit wealth into your hands. You have to get wisdom of how to take possession of the land and manage the land once you gain it. That's the only way that the wealth of the wicked will be transferred into the hands of the righteous, because God will not put wealth into irresponsible hands. God will not put wealth into irresponsible hands, even if those hands are of the righteous. God doesn't appreciate waste. Therefore, if you want to qualify for wealth, then, God expects you to aggressively learn how to obtain and manage wealth. Again, Proverbs 24: 3-4 says,

> 3. Through wisdom is an house built; and by understanding it is established:

> 4. And by knowledge shall the chambers be filled with all precious and pleasant riches.

Also, Proverbs 13:22 says,

> 22. A good man leaveth an inheritance to his children's children: and the wealth of the sinner is laid up for the just.

Wealth is "laid up for the just." Yet, "the just" has to do what's necessary to take possession of it by aggressively seeking and getting knowledge. Proverbs 24: 4 says,

> 4. And by knowledge shall the chambers be filled with all precious and pleasant riches.

Again, Proverbs 13:23 says,

> 23. Much food is in the tillage of the poor: but there is that is destroyed for want of judgment.

Knowledge Is The Key To Riches

There is much food, resources, provisions, etc., which are derived from the work of the poor. The only thing that is lacking is the knowledge of how to maximize, possess, and manage it. Some of the poorest people in the world are the hardest working people. They break down their bodies, their minds, and their souls while working hard, but they lack the knowledge of how to maximize their efforts. They lack the knowledge of how to capitalize on their ideas. They lack the knowledge of how to get the most out of their efforts so that they have something left over for their children and grandchildren. They lack the knowledge of how to work "smart" so as to be preserved in their bodies to enjoy their latter years. Again, Proverbs 13:23 says,

> 23. Much food is in the tillage of the poor: but there is that is destroyed for want of judgment.

In other words, "Much food is in the tillage of the poor: but there is that is destroyed (or wasted, or stolen, or pillaged) for want of judgment (or knowledge). Hosea 4: 6 says,

> 6. My people are destroyed for lack of knowledge: because thou hast rejected knowledge, I will also reject thee, that thou shalt be no priest to me: seeing thou hast forgotten the law of thy God.

This is God talking to His people. He is talking to those who are saved. He is talking to those who know the Lord as Savior. He is talking to those who are sanctified. He is talking to those who have been praying, loving their neighbor as they love themselves, and worshipping of God. However, the only thing that is lacking according to Hosea 4:6 is "knowledge."

> 6. My people are destroyed for lack of knowledge: because thou hast rejected knowledge, I will also reject thee, that thou shalt be no priest to me: seeing thou hast forgotten the law of thy God.

"Lack of knowledge" not only jeopardizes your life and future provision, but it also jeopardizes your family's provision. A learning family is a leading family. A leading family is a learning family. Again, "My people are destroyed for lack of knowledge . . ." (Hosea 4:6). Therefore, the increase of knowledge helps to stop destruction. Instruction stops destruction. You equip yourself to prevent loss and destruction in your life and family by gaining knowledge. You first need to learn God's biblical principles of finance regarding tithing. You also want to gain other practical knowledge for living. You want to get knowledge and wisdom in every area. Again, Proverbs 24: 3-4 says,

> 3. Through wisdom is an house built; and by understanding it is established:

4. And by knowledge shall the chambers be filled with all precious and pleasant riches.

The only way that you get "precious and pleasant riches" in your house is through knowledge. The only way that you are going to pay off your house is by knowledge. You need to get the "know-how." If you don't "know-how", then, you need to find out "how?" You need to get some "know-how." Once your home is established in marriage, then, the goal of your family should be to increase in wisdom, knowledge, and "know-how", so that your family can become financially free. This is a very critical key to help you "GAIN 20/20 VISION FOR THE NEW DECADE! A Step By Step Path To A More Successful Future.

CHAPTER FIVE

Health: The 3rd Essential Key To A More Successful New Decade

In this section of the book I would like to help you "GAIN 20/20 VISION FOR THE NEW DECADE!" in the area of "Health." Proverbs 3:1–8 reveals to us the foundation for a healthy, successful living. You can have success in every area, but if you don't have success in your health, then, everything else is compromised, because you can't enjoy it. In 3 John 2, God tells us all that He desires for us. He says, "Beloved, I wish above all things that you prosper and be in health, even as your soul prospers." That's His desire above everything else. That simplifies matters for us. God says, "My bottom-line for you, out of all your going to church, praying, and singing, and giving tithes and offerings, and walking in love, etc., is that you "prosper, be in health, even as your soul prosper." Out of all the scripture that you read, and all the preaching that you've heard, God says, "This is what I want for you ultimately. I want you to 'prosper, be in health, even as your soul prospers.'" "Prosper" means "to succeed, to advance, to go forward, to increase materially, and to increase in enjoyment in life." God also says He wants you to "be in health." He doesn't only want you to "be healed." Rather, God desires that you not suffer sicknesses. Nevertheless, God does promise you that "I Am the Lord, your God, that healeth you" (Exodus 15:26). So, if do need healing, God promises that "I Am the Lord, your God, that healeth you" (Exodus 15:26). He's continually healing you. He's restoring your youth like the eagles. He's restoring your health. He's restoring your soul. God is your redeemer. He is your restorer. He renews your health. He brings healing to you. Furthermore, He says, "I want you to abide in a healthy condition." So, God says, "All of the dietary laws of scripture is for you to have good health. I want you to have good heart health. I want your arteries clear of any clogs, so that you have good circulation and good blood flow throughout your body. I want your blood pressure to be stable at 120/80. I want your sugar levels to be perfect in your body. I want you to be stress free. I want you to be in health." Therefore, God gives us certain dietary laws in scripture. However, it is the natural and the supernatural that brings us divine health. Walking in love brings about health. Keeping a heart free from anger, un-forgiveness, and malice and strife, helps you keep a peaceful heart. This brings health to the soul. It brings health to the body. Peace in your heart brings restoration. However, if you're bound up with emotional bile, guile, and vitriol inside of you, then, it's poisoning your physical body. Strife, malice, and grudges poison your body and it diminishes your health. So, God says in 3 John 2, "Beloved, I wish above all things that you prosper, and be in health, even as your soul prospers." God desires that you abide in a state of good health. God wants your immune system healthy. However, if you get emotionally distraught, or in emotional turmoil and anger, then, it can break down your immune system, so that, when you go out into the public, where there are germs and viruses, it makes you more susceptible to sicknesses and diseases, because your emotional state will cause your physical resistance to those diseases to be broken down. And, the blood cells in your immune system that would normally be strong for fighting viruses and germs will be weakened if you're not emotionally sound. Then, you can open yourself up to sicknesses and diseases. If you're carrying offense inside of your heart, such as un-forgiveness, regret, continual sorrow, etc., then, all of that is pulling down your natural defenses. It's breaking down your bones. It's negatively affecting your blood formulation in your bone marrow. Your physical health is being impacted by what's going on internally. Therefore, to "Gain 20/20 Vision For The New Decade! A Step By Step Path To A More Successful Future" starts off with your relationship with God. If you keep your relationship with God in the proper place, then, you will have overall success. God evaluates the heart. Everything starts from the heart. Good health starts in the heart. Jesus said, "Out of the abundance of the heart the mouth speaketh" (Matthew 12:34). Proverbs says "Keep thy heart with all diligence; for out of it are the issues of life" (Proverbs 4:23). What "issues forth" from your heart will be what your life becomes. So, success and prosperity issues forth from the heart. It starts in the heart. Proverbs says, "As a man thinketh in his heart, so is he . . ." (Proverbs 23:7a) God gave King Solomon "largeness of heart, even as the sand of the sea shore" (1 Kings 4:29). He had a prosperous heart. He had room for God to fill his heart with prosperity, and, thus, he "made silver and gold as stones in Israel" (2 Chronicle 1:15). King Solomon had a prosperous heart. Therefore, he had a prosperous life. Therefore, if you have healthy thoughts, then, you will have a healthier life. If you think positive, life-giving thoughts, and have positive words and actions, then, you will have a more positive life. Health is often a matter of thoughts, words, and actions. It comes from the heart. God always evaluates our heart. Therefore, good heart health begins with reverence of God. If you truly reverence God, then, you will always be conscious of what's going on in your heart. Because, you know that the Holy Spirit lives inside of your heart, thus, you are always watchful of what you allow in your heart. If you are someone who truly reverences God, then, you are always heart conscious. Why? Because, you know that the Holy Spirit hears the thoughts of your heart. He hears the words of your mouth. And, He evaluates the intent of your heart concerning your actions. Your relationship with God, with others, and yourself, impacts your health. 3 John 2 says, "Beloved, I wish above all things that you may prosper and be in health, even as your soul prospers." God wishes that you prosper to the same degree or parallel to the degree of your soul prosperity. Your soul is your mind, will, emotions, intellect, disposition, and personality. You can prosper in each one of these areas. You can develop greater growth and refinement in each of these areas of the soul. "Prosper" means "to advance, to go forward, and to increase." Prosper means "to mature." In other words, God wants you to grow into the full stature of someone that's made in the image and likeness of God. He wants you to grow into the full stature of a son or daughter of God. He wants you to grow into the full stature of being God's direct offspring. He wants you to grow into the full stature of being God's representative on Earth. He wants you to grow into the full stature of someone who demonstrates the ways, thoughts, and manners of God on Earth. He wants you to be a demonstration of a human being filled with God. God wants you to come into the full stature of a human being submitted to the Holy Spirit.

You Are God's Representative

A few years ago, in popular culture, the question was asked "*What Would Jesus Do?*" There was wrist bands made with the reminder "WWJD" to help the person wearing it to consider what Jesus would do in any given situation. This was a great idea and tool for considering how we should respond to life. Someone should be able to look at your life and see what Jesus would do. Someone should be able to look at your life and see what God would think or say in a particular situation. 3 John 2 says, "Beloved, I wish above all things that you may prosper and be in health, even as your soul prospers." Your soul is your mind (you should think like God by renewing your mind), your will (you should want the same things that God wants), your emotions (you should demonstrate the fruit of the spirit and you be emotionally stable), your personality (you should demonstrate the nature of God), your intellect, and your disposition (you have the understanding and personality of God). Thus, people should be able to *sense* that God lives in you. So, you should ask throughout your day "Am I acting like God? Is this a feeling that God would have? Is this something that God would do?" If not, then, you should cast it off. You should "lay aside every weight and sin that so easily beset us or trip you up. And, run with patience the race that is set before you, looking unto Jesus the author and finisher of your faith" (Hebrews 12:1-3). Jesus was in a body just like us. He overcame temptation in a body just like us. He did it for us so that He could understand our challenges and give us the grace to be victorious just like He was. Proverbs 3:1-8 gives us the foundation for healthy living. It is only through obeying God's principles that we will obtain successful living. This is what it says:

---

1. My son, forget not my law; but let thine heart keep my commandments:

2. For length of days, and long life, and peace, shall they add to thee.

3. Let not mercy and truth forsake thee: bind them about thine neck; write them upon the table of thine heart:

4. So shalt thou find favor and good understanding in the sight of God and man.

Through seeking the mercy and truth of God, you will obtain favor and good understanding in the sight of God and man. Why? It is because, you will always be living your life conscious of whether you're following after God's mercy and walking in His truth.

> 5. Trust in the Lord with all thine heart; and lean not unto thine own understanding.

Simply live according to what God's Word says in every situation.

> 6. In all thy ways acknowledge him, and he shall direct thy paths.

Keep casting your care upon the Lord and He will direct your path. Proverbs 16:3 also says "Commit your works unto the Lord and your thoughts shall be established".

---

7. Be not wise in thine own eyes: fear the Lord, and depart from evil.

By simply casting our cares upon the Lord and trusting God with every area of our life, then, we are relieved of the burden of life. We have been given authority in the earth. However, it is delegated authority. Ultimately, the power and responsibility belongs to God. You can be strong in the Lord and in the power of His might. Not your own might or power. Good health starts with relieving our heart of the burdens of life, and rather, depending on God for your life. Ephesians 6: 10-18 encourages us to depend on the power and authority of God for victory in life. This is what it says,

> 10. Finally, my brethren, be strong in the Lord, and in the power of his might.

God wants you to be strong in life. However, it comes from your continued reliance upon the Lord. The following verses tells you how to do it:

> 11. Put on the whole armour of God, that ye may be able to stand against the wiles of the devil.

God tells us to put on the whole armor of God in order to have protection and strength against the attacks of the devil in this life.

> 12. For we wrestle not against flesh and blood, but against principalities, against powers, against the rulers of the darkness of this world, against spiritual wickedness in high places.

We're in a "wrestling match" against the adversity of life in the world. We must be prepared with God's strength and protection in order to successfully overcome and resist what is coming against us.

> 13. Wherefore take unto you the whole armour of God, that ye may be able to withstand in the evil day, and having done all, to stand.

The scripture says, "having done all, to stand". We have to do all that's required to "withstand" the pressure, worry, opposition, etc., of life.

14. Stand therefore, having your loins girt about with truth, and having on the breastplate of righteousness;

15. And your feet shod with the preparation of the gospel of peace;

16. Above all, taking the shield of faith, wherewith ye shall be able to quench all the fiery darts of the wicked.

17. And take the helmet of salvation, and the sword of the Spirit, which is the word of God.

18. Praying always with all prayer and supplication in the Spirit, and watching thereunto with all perseverance and supplication for all saints.

This passage gives the equipment necessary to protect our soul from the assaults of the flesh, the world, and the devil. Thereby, our health will be protected. Proverbs 3:8 says

8. It shall be health to thy navel, and marrow to thy bones.

God's Word Adds Life To Your Life

God lets us know that His Word is the source of health and long life. The Bible says in Proverbs 3:2, "For length of days, and long life, and peace, shall they add to thee." God promises that as we obey His Word and His principles for living, it will extend our life, increase our health, and give us peace. In fact, God promises us that obeying His Word will actually "add" days and years to our life.

God's Word teaches us how to treat people. How we treat people greatly affects the length of our life. If you walk in peace, forgiveness, and love towards other people, then, you will extend your heart health. Your blood flow will be more normal and natural. Your blood pressure will be more stable. Your blood will be healthier and disease-free. Your body will be less inclined toward cancers, viruses, tumors, and other disorders. Walking in peace and forgiveness towards others puts you at peace with God. God lives in your spirit. Each person was created by God, and, thus, is a part of God. God is life. As you treat people well, you are in agreement with life. Thus, your life will be increased as you maintain peace with other people, who are connected to the source of all life, which is God. So, as you treat other people well, then, you are treating God well. You become a maintainer of peace with life. This increases your health and life. Treating people well increases your "favor and good understanding in the sight of God and man" (Proverbs 3:4). As you walk through life in favor and good understanding in the sight of God and man, you will have less stress. You will feel good about your life. You will feel good about others, and others will feel good about you. There will be less friction, contention, and strife in your life, and thus, your heart will be healthier, your body will be less stressed, and your circulation will be more normal. You will have healthier bones and joints, thus decreasing the likelihood of debilitating arthritis. Your physical health is often connected to your emotional state. You will be at peace emotionally. Proverbs 3:5-8 says,

> 5. Trust in the Lord with all thine heart; and lean not unto thine own understanding.
>
> 6. In all thy ways acknowledge him, and he shall direct thy paths.
>
> 7. Be not wise in thine own eyes: fear the Lord, and depart from evil.
>
> 8. It shall be health to thy navel, and marrow to thy bones.

God lets us know that trusting in Him is the source of peace. If you go through life with a sense of knowing that God is for you, with you, and in you, then, you will be less stressed. As you live your life continually in relationship with God through prayer, Bible study, singing praises and worship, and just acknowledging Him throughout the day, then, you will have more peace of mind. That will increase and enhance your health. You will carry a lighter load through life. You will not be burdened down in life. The Bible says in Proverbs 3:8 "It shall be health to thy navel, and marrow to thy bones." In other words, the center of your being shall spring forth with good health, and your blood, which is produced in the marrow of your bones, will be healthy and disease free. This is a key to helping you "GAIN 20/20 VISION FOR THE NEW DECADE! A Step By Step Path To A More Successful Future." It starts with our relationship with God. Also, success in life is depended upon having a healthy marriage and peace in our other relationships. It is critical to have good health to truly have success in the new decade.

CHAPTER SIX

Finance: The 4th Essential Key To A More Successful New Decade

We have discussed three critical areas in your "Step By Step Path To A More Successful Future." We discussed your relationship with 1) God. We discussed how to have success in your 2) Marriage & Family. We have discussed the importance of having divine 3) Health. Now, Proverbs 8:17–21 shares God's will for your finances. It's God's will that you be healthy, wealthy, and wise. This is what it says:

---

17. I love them that love me; and those that seek me early shall find me.

18. Riches and honor are with me; yes, durable riches and righteousness.

19. My fruit is better than gold, yes, than fine gold; and my revenue than choice silver.

20. I lead in the way of righteousness, in the midst of the paths of judgment:

21. That I may cause those that love me to inherit substance; and I will fill their treasures.

Seek God Early and You Will Find Him

The word "early" means diligently. The word early actually means "early" in a practical sense. It is speaking of people who rise up early to seek the Lord. It is speaking of people who rise up early to *"break the dawn"* with the Lord. People who rise up early to seek God in prayer to start their day will find the Lord. You can take this figuratively. However, this is literal as well. People who get up early in the morning seeking God in a devotion of Bible reading, worship, and prayer will find the Lord. There are some things that the Lord will reveal to you in the *still* of the morning that you may not get at other times. There's a song that says, "I come to the garden alone, while the dew is still on the roses, and the joy that we share, as we tarry there. No other has ever known. And, He walks with me, and He talks with me, and He tells me I am His own."

This is literal. This key will help you "GAIN 20/20 VISION FOR THE NEW DECADE! A Step By Step Path To A More Successful Future." This is a real strategy. Proverbs 8: 17 says,

> 17. I love them that love me; and those that seek me early shall find me.

Seeking God in the early part of the morning is a key. Many successful business people wake up early to do their reading, devotions, affirmations, meditations, and exercises in order to get their mind clear while it's still quiet, and before the other energy of the day starts. They start very early before all of the other activity and spiritual activity of the day starts, so that they can hear clearly and get clarity in their minds. Many times they will find answers and strategies for their day in the *still* of the morning. So, this is a real strategy. The personification of wisdom speaks to us in Proverbs 8:30 and says,

> 30. Then I was by him, as one brought up with him: and I was daily his delight, rejoicing always before him;

> 31. Rejoicing in the habitable part of his earth; and my delights were with the sons of men.

So, God's wisdom says that He "delights" in spending time with us. If you're willing to spend time with God and His wisdom, then, His wisdom delights to spend time with you. God delights to reveal Himself to mankind. God delights to reveal answers to you. God delights to give you insights. God delights to show you the way that you should live. God delights to give you strategies to be successful. God delights to give you answers to your health concerns. God delights to give strategies and answers for your family concerns. God delights to give you answers for your job concerns. He delights in spending time with you. If you will spend time with Him, then, He will spend time with you. Proverbs 8:31 says,

> 31. Rejoicing in the habitable part of his earth; and my delights were with the sons of men.

God's Wisdom rejoiced to spend time with mankind in the "habitable part of his earth." Jesus is the personification of Wisdom. Now, He's giving us instruction in Proverbs 8:32, it says,

> 32. Now therefore hearken unto me, O ye children: for blessed are they that keep my ways.
>
> 33. Hear instruction, and be wise, and refuse it not.
>
> 34. Blessed is the man that heareth me, watching daily at my gates, waiting at the posts of my doors.

You should seek God daily. You should daily watch at His gates. You should do this early in the morning. You should look for Him. Jesus is Wisdom. You should go seeking Him early in the morning. You should schedule a time early in the morning to seek the Lord and hear what He has to say for that day. You should "watch" when Wisdom comes "walking by." It is like Wisdom is coming walking through the city and He has answers for your day. He has answers to provide for "whosoever will, let them come." "Let them receive of His wisdom." But, you have to be "watching". You have to be watching when He walks out of the doors of Heaven early in the morning into Earth. God seeks to reveal Himself to us. He comes daily seeking to find someone that is receptive to His wisdom. God is a gracious Father and King. He wants to share Himself with us His children. He tells us to seek Him daily. He wants us to be successful in life. He wants our lives to be prosperous and abundant on Earth. God has an abundance of guidance and counsel for those that make it their lifestyle to seek Him. No matter what you are facing, you can be certain that God is there to answer you and help you. You should seek His counsel daily about every area of your life. You can cast your cares and concerns on God. Jesus is the gracious Lord, our Shepherd. He is committed to helping you successfully make your journey through life. You never have to feel alone. You always have access to the wisdom and guidance of God. All you have to do is make it your habit and custom to seek Him daily. Seek Him early. He will always guide your days. God is gracious. He loves you. He loves your family. He is concerned about your health. He is concerned about your finances. He has answers for every area of your life. Proverbs 8:34 says,

> 34. Blessed is the man that heareth me, watching daily at my gates, waiting at the posts of my doors.

You must be watching early when Wisdom comes walking out of the "gates" of the city of Heaven into Earth going on His daily journey. You should be watching and waiting as Wisdom comes through the "posts of His doors" so that you can *tag along* and walk along with Him and get those answers that you need for your life. Proverbs 13: 20a says,

> 20a. He that walketh with wise men shall be wise . . .

You should seek God daily. You should seek to walk with Jesus along the journey of life. He hears every prayer that you whisper to Him. The person that walks with Jesus shall be wise. That man, woman, boy, girl, or teenager who walks with Him and talks with Him and fellowships early with Him, you shall be empowered with wisdom. You shall be endued with knowledge. You shall be endued with revelation. Proverbs 8:34 says,

---

> 34. Blessed is the man that heareth me, watching daily at my gates, waiting at the posts of my doors.

You should make seeking God your daily habit. "Daily" means you do it everyday. That means that you have a custom of seeking the Lord. You have a habit of seeking the Lord. He comes walking out of His gates early in the morning. He comes walking past the "posts of his doors" early in the morning before the hustle and bustle of the day starts. He walks out early before something else highjacks your brain, highjacks your mind, and highjacks your emotions. Wisdom walks out early before all of the trouble, before all of the concerns, before the rest of the family wakes up with all of their concerns, before the worries, and before the devil can highjack your morning with all of the stress, concerns, and, anxiety. You need to wake up early and beat the devil to the punch. You need to go fall on your knees before God and read the Bible and pray and seek Him early by "watching daily at His gates and waiting at the posts of His doors". Proverbs 8:35 continues,

> 35. For whoso findeth me findeth life, and shall obtain favour of the Lord.

Therefore, it's a search. In other words, "the person who captures God", the person who captures Jesus, is the person who captures Wisdom as He "walks out of the door." Wisdom is a prize. Wisdom is a possession. To have the opportunity to talk to the source of all wisdom is a prized possession. One of the things that you obtain when you get the wisdom of God for your day is "favor." You gain "life." However, Proverbs 8:36 says,

> 36. But he that sinneth against me wrongeth his own soul: all they that hate me love death.

Seek God Diligently

Now, look back at Proverbs 8:17.

> 17. I love them that love me; and those that seek me early shall find me.

"Early" has several meanings. "Early" is a time of day. "Early" also means "diligently, wholeheartedly, and earnestly." Furthermore, generally, many people that wake up early to start a job or task or to arrive at their job early or study early are typically considered diligent. It's not always the case that people who rise up later are not diligent when they finally get up, however, people who get up early display a characteristic that they are diligent and earnest about what they are about to do. It displays that they really want to do it. They really want to see it come to pass. They really want to get the jump on it. Proverbs 8:17 says again,

> 17. I love them that love me; and those that seek me early shall find me.

"Early" means diligently or earnestly. Another meaning of "early" in the Hebrew is to "break the dawn." When I was a child growing up my Grandfather gave me and my brothers a couple of specific instructions: He said, "It shouldn't take a man no longer than fifteen minutes to be ready to go anywhere." He was talking to us about being ready. He didn't want us to be taking a long time to get dressed and ready to go places when he came by to pick us up. Therefore, he said, "It shouldn't take a man no longer than fifteen minutes to go anywhere." In other words, "You should already have your clothes ready. You should already have your clothes laid out the night before. You should be able to jump in and out of the shower, put on your deodorant, brush your hair, brush your teeth, and get out of the door." Secondly, my Grandfather said, "Never let the Sun meet you in the face." In other words, "Never let the Sun meet you while you're still laying in the bed and greet you in the face." Rather, you should already be up when the Sun rises. When the Sun rises, then, you should meet it by already being up out of the bed. That was a good word of advice and wisdom. My Grandfather was in the military in his younger years. So, I'm sure he had to practice certain disciplines that required him to be ready "on the spot." They had to eat and get done with their food. They couldn't have those long, relaxing, luxurious meals of sitting around drinking lemonade and talking for long periods of time. Rather, they had to down their grub and be ready to go. Those are instructions that I learned from my Grandfather. I remind myself of those things in order to live a more successful and wise life. These types of instructions will help you "GAIN 20/20 VISION FOR THE NEW DECADE! A Step By Step Path To More Successful Future."

Blessings Come From Diligence

Again Proverbs 8:17-21 begins to say the following,

> 17. I love them that love me; and those that seek me early shall find me.

The first step for you to "Gain 20/20 Vision For The New Decade!" is your relationship with God. Every other blessing comes from your relationship with God.

> 18. Riches and honour are with me; yea, durable riches and righteousness.

God promises the person who practices the lifestyle of seeking Him early will obtain "riches and honour." The person who seeks His wisdom early by "waiting at the posts of His doors" to seek Him in prayer, Bible study, and worship, will be taught the wisdom of God. Sometimes God will reveal it to you in the Word. Sometimes He will lead you by His Spirit. Sometimes He won't say very much. Rather, He will lead you to a book. He will say, "Open that book. Your answer is in that book." So, He won't tell you. He will make you search for it. He will make you read it and study it. He will give you direction. However, He will put you on a "chase" to find and seek wisdom. Proverbs 4:7 says,

> 7. Wisdom is the principal thing; therefore get wisdom: and with all thy getting get understanding.

So, oftentimes, you have to go on the "chase." For example, if you want to be a doctor, then, you've got to go to medical school. If you want to be a lawyer, then, you've got to go to law school. There are some things that are only found in the books that people have already learned and recorded. Yet, the principles will remain the same. Therefore, Proverbs 4:7 says, "Wisdom is the principal thing, therefore get wisdom, and with all your getting get understanding." However, there is certain knowledge that you have to seek out in order to gain the advantage and prosperity out of life. Nevertheless, in order to "GAIN 20/20 VISION FOR THE NEW DECADE! A Step By Step Path To A More Successful Future" starts with your relationship with 1) God. The Bible says, "The fear of the Lord is the beginning of wisdom". The reverence of God is the foundation. Proverbs 8:17-21 says,

17. I love them that love me; and those that seek me early shall find me.

"Early" means early in the day, early in life, or diligently. It pays to seek God early. Godly "Riches and honour" comes from seeking God. In other words, God says, "As you walk with me through life and follow my principles, then, riches and honour are with me." The phrase "with me" means you are on a journey with God. As you seek God diligently on your journey you will find riches and honour. He says that you will obtain "durable riches." "Durable riches" are riches that *last*. Land is an example of durable riches. No matter whether the real estate market goes up or down, the land is still going to be of value, because land is a limited resource. God is not making any more land. He is not adding more earth to the Earth. So, if you have real estate, then, that's "durable riches." All of the natural resources that are on your land are durable riches. What you build on your land, such as houses are durable riches. The gold is durable riches. Gold and silver has always been valuable. Oil and other natural resources are durable riches. Industries that are a part of the commerce system of a society is durable riches. Businesses, financial, and transportation systems are durable riches. The utilities are durable riches. Proverbs 8:18 says,

18. Riches and honour are with me;
yea, durable riches and righteousness.

19. My fruit is better than gold, yea,
than fine gold; and my revenue than
choice silver.

God says, "He will make sure that you have durable riches and that you will be righteous and upright." God says, "That which will come out your lifestyle of seeking My Word and learning My ways, and having My Word rooted in your heart is better than gold." Jesus said in the parable of the "Sower" in the Gospels that the "Sower soweth the Word." The Word is a seed. You sow the seed in your heart. You are the "good ground." You sow the seed of the Word in your heart. You bring forth "good fruit" after a matter of time. The outgrowth of you fellowshipping with God is "better than gold." It's better than financial gain. God's wisdom brings life to you. It brings healing to you. It brings eternal life. It brings wholeness to you. It blesses your family. God says that the outgrowth of your relationship with Him is "better than gold." Yet, He says, "I'm still going to give you the gold."

19. My fruit is better than gold, yea, than fine gold; and my revenue than choice silver.

God says, "You're going to gain revenue, but the revenue that you gain from me is better than choice silver." God says, not only does He want you to be financially rich, but He also wants you to be enriched in the other areas of your life. He wants you to be enriched through your relationship with Him. He wants you to be enriched by your experience with Him. God wants you to be a richer person. He wants you to be a wiser person. He wants you to be a wealthier person. The result of your relationship with God will be that you are a wise person, you are a healthy person, you are a wholesome person, you are a strong person, you are a godly person, you are made in the image and likeness of God, you demonstrate His character, and you are a blessed person. Wherever you go is blessed. You speak the Blessing. The Blessing of the Lord makes you rich and He adds no sorrow with it. It's not just the riches that make you rich. Rather, it's the manifested, declared Blessing of the Lord that makes you rich. You are the blessed of the Lord.

You Have Been Enriched

19. My fruit is better than gold, yea, than fine gold; and my revenue than choice silver.

God says, "The fruit of the seed of My Word that has been planted in you is that you have become enriched. The result of your relationship with me is that you have become enriched." You have been blessed with the favor of God. He says, "I will make you rich. However, I'm also going to enrich you." Wherever you go will be prosperous. Whoever you talk to will be blessed. Whoever you come around will become blessed. Wherever you become employed will be blessed because you are there. Your neighborhood is blessed because you are there. Your children are blessed wherever they go. You shall decree a thing and it is established in the earth because you have the blessing of the Lord. You have the favor of the Lord. You are the Blessed of the Lord. You have been enriched.

19. My fruit is better than gold, yea,
than fine gold; and my revenue than
choice silver.

20. I lead in the way of righteousness,
in the midst of the paths of judgment.

You have been on a journey. The Blessing of God is the result of a lifestyle. This is your lifestyle of walking with God in the earth. You're not alone. You're not in the world without God and without hope. No. You have God on the inside. You're inside of God and God is inside of you. In Acts 17:28, it says, "For in Him we live, and move, and have our being . . . For are also His offspring". Hallelujah! God surround us. We are in Him and He is in us.

20. I lead in the way of righteousness,
in the midst of the paths of judgment:

So, He's leading you on a journey. King David says in Psalm 23,

1. The Lord is my shepherd; I shall not want.

2. He maketh me to lie down in green pastures: he leadeth me beside the still waters.

3. He restoreth my soul: he leadeth me in the paths of righteousness for his name's sake.

4. Yea, though I walk through the valley of the shadow of death, I will fear no evil: for thou art with me; thy rod and thy staff they comfort me.

5. Thou preparest a table before me in the presence of mine enemies: thou anointest my head with oil; my cup runneth over.

6. Surely goodness and mercy shall
follow me all the days of my life: and
I will dwell in the house of the Lord
for ever.

Hallelujah! This is a lifestyle. God surrounds you. You're in His presence. He's with you. He's for you. He's in you. He's enriched you! You're enriched in your relationship with God. This is how you "GAIN 20/20 VISION FOR THE NEW DECADE! A Step By Step Path To A More Successful Future." Proverbs 8:20 says,

---

20. I lead in the way of righteousness,
in the midst of the paths of judgment.

God helps you to make good decisions. He leads in the way of being and doing right in the earth. He puts you in the middle of the path to make "good sense" decisions and choices. He will bless you if you go to the right or to the left, north or south, east or west, and wherever you have set your foot, because He's given you the Blessing! You're the blessed of the Lord. He's enriched you, because you have been spending time with Him. He's guiding you and giving you wisdom. Proverbs 8:21 continues to say why He's been leading you,

---

21. That I may cause those that love me to inherit substance; and I will fill their treasures.

"Substance" is wealth. If you don't understand "substance" as meaning wealth, then, hopefully, you understand "treasures" as meaning wealth. You know that "treasures" are something of value. For example, you have the United States Treasury. It has financial assets in it that are heavily guarded, because it is very valuable.

God says, "You will inherit substance, which is your birthright, because you have been honoring me with your finances through giving tithes and offerings." For example, Abraham had been honoring God with his finances through giving tithes and offerings. When he met up with Melchizidek, after he won the battle and rescued his nephew Lot, he gave tithes of all the spoils that he gained from the battle in order to say, "I'm in covenant with God. Everything I gain in life I will honor God with, in order to acknowledge that I know that it came from Him." Therefore, inheriting substance is your birthright. Inheriting substance is your birthright. Substance means wealth, property, land, cattle, gold, silver, employees, businesses, etc. God says, "I will cause those that love me to inherit substance." God says, "Because you have been walking with me and following after me as your lifestyle, then, you will inherit substance." I remember growing up in church. The saints used to be serious about God. The saints use to be *on fire* for God. They would seek God early in the morning. They would wake up early in the morning to pray and read the Bible. They wouldn't leave their house without praying. They would be on their break at work and have their little New Testament with the Psalms and Proverbs. They would go in the restroom and read a couple of scriptures and ask the

Lord to guide them. They would ask the Lord to "Please guide me in what to say. Please give me wisdom." The saints use to be *on fire* for the Lord. They use to love the Lord. That was love. They used to love the Lord. But, now, often, the saints have become lax. The saints have become lethargic. The saints have become apathetic. The saints have become diluted in their passion for God. The saints have become disappointed and disengaged. But, the saints use to be on fire for the Lord. And, also, during that time you use to see the power of God manifest greater too. You would see healing in the marketplace. You would see people get delivered on the streets. You would see people get saved at the workplace. You would see people get saved on the bus. You would see people get saved in the grocery store. You would see the devil cast out in the church. You would see bodies healed. The saints were on fire back then. The saints thought that Jesus was coming soon. The saints were saying, "Jesus is coming soon." They said, "Jesus is on the mainline. Tell Him what you want." The saints were calling on Jesus. The saints knew that they needed Jesus back then. But, now, the saints are not seeking Jesus with that same passion. Proverbs 8:21 says,

> 21. That I may cause those that love me to inherit substance; and I will fill their treasures

You "inherit" substance because you are His child. However, Joseph inherited a "double portion", because of the way he honored God and his father, Jacob. His brothers inherited their regular portion. Yet, Joseph received a "double portion" because of the honor that he gave to his father Jacob. God says, "I love them that love me" (Proverbs 8:17). God says, "I honor them that honor me, and they that despise me shall be lightly esteemed" (1 Samuel 2:30). Again, Proverbs 8:17-21 says,

> 17. I love them that love me; and those that seek me early shall find me.
>
> 18. Riches and honour are with me; yea, durable riches and righteousness.

19. My fruit is better than gold, yea,
than fine gold; and my revenue than
choice silver.

20. I lead in the way of righteousness,
in the midst of the paths of judgment:

Again, the word "early" means diligently. God says, "Riches and honor are with me." He is saying, "The riches and honor that I give you, you're not going to get it without me." He says, "The riches and honor are with me." The riches and honor that God gives, you won't get it without Him. So, you need to walk with Him. You need to seek Him "early". You need to seek Him diligently. You need to be "watching at His gates" and "the posts of His doors" early in the morning, because the "riches and honor" are with Him. God will show you how to get it and how to be "righteous" when you get it. The "outgrowth" of your relationship with God is "better than gold". God "leads" in the way of making right decisions. God "leads" in the way of doing the right thing. Even when you don't know exactly what to do at the time, God says, He will put you right in the middle surrounded by choices of good decisions. Whatever path you go in, I'm going to be leading you in the path of judgment. Sometimes you don't know exactly what to do in a situation. Sometimes the answer may not be clear. Sometimes you may not have gotten a Word on it or heard the voice of God on it. Yet, in Psalm 16: 5-11

God promises to lead us. This is what King David says about God's promise to lead us,

> 5. The Lord is the portion of mine inheritance and of my cup: thou maintainest my lot.
>
> 6. The lines are fallen unto me in pleasant places; yea, I have a goodly heritage.
>
> 7. I will bless the Lord, who hath given me counsel: my reins also instruct me in the night seasons.

The word "cup" in the Hebrew means "purse or money bag." He says, "God is my bank account, my inheritance, my savings, and God is my pocket money. God blesses my purse and "money-bag." God is my daily provision. He's my inheritance. He's my pension. He's my 401k. He's my Social Security fund. Also, He's my daily money. He watches over my investments and inheritance in spite of the economy. So, David is saying, "God has cut me off a nice chuck of property for my inheritance. I've got a river or stream on my property. I've got some fruit trees on my land. I have plenty of greenery for my cattle." The children of Israel divided the "good land" of Canaan according to their tribes. David said, "The lines have fallen unto me in pleasant places. I've got some rivers on my land. I've got some fruit trees. I've got some valleys for my cattle. I've got some copper and gold on my land. I've got oil on my land." God puts you in "paths of judgment", because you have been walking with Him. You have been seeking Him early. You have been seeking Him diligently. So, God leads you even in the "night seasons" when you can't see with your natural eyes. Because you have renewed your mind to the Spirit of the Word, the Holy Spirit can still lead you internally concerning what to do in the paths of good sense, even when it doesn't make sense to your natural mind. He says, "My reins also instruct me in the night seasons" (Psalm 16:7). In other words, "My *guts* instruct me when I can't see clearly with my mind." God can give you a "gut feeling" concerning the right thing to do now. You can say, "My heart is telling me to do this or that. I feel it on the inside that this is the right thing to do. I'm discerning that this is the right thing to do." Someone may ask you "What evidence do you have?" And, you will answer them, "Well, I just have a feeling that everything is going to be alright if I take this step. I believe that this is the way that God is leading me. I can sense that God is guiding me to do this now. I believe that this is the time." It's obscure. It's dark. Yet, you have been spending enough time with God over the years that you can sense His ways. He has put you in the path of judgment and good sense. Why can you trust this kind of instinct to make the right decisions in these cases? You have developed a relationship of seeking God. You have been seeking Him early. You have a morning routine. You wake up every morning early and seek God for wisdom and answers in the Word, in prayer, and in worship for that day. You may not have gotten all of the answers. You didn't read every scripture in the Bible in order to find an answer. You may have just gotten a core scripture and got that nugget for the day and got your instructions. And, you go out and start your day. You don't know what the day holds. You don't know exactly every person you're going to come in contact with. You don't know what kind of questions, situations, circumstances, or attitudes you're going to be confronted with. You don't know all of that. Yet, you have a routine of seeking God's Word everyday early and following after Him so that He can lead you in the paths of judgment. He can lead you in the paths of good sense. Your "reins" can "instruct" you in the "night seasons." This is how you "GAIN 20/20 VISION FOR THE NEW DECADE! A Step By Step Path To A More Successful Future." We are now looking at key 4) Finances. It's good to have the leading of the Lord concerning your finances. Whether you're in business, on your job, as a student in school, as a parent, etc. It's good to have the leading of the Lord. It's good to know that God is with you.

In other words, "Because God is with me and I have been seeking Him. Therefore, I don't leave His presence." So, even when you can't see clearly, yet, you still know that God is directing you. He's with you. He can lead you. They that are led by the Spirit are the sons of God. They that are led by the Spirit are the mature of the Lord. He doesn't always have to give you a special Word. Nor, does God have to send you an angel for you to know that He has a message for you. He doesn't have to show you a rainbow in the sky to confirm every intention of His heart for you. No. He can lead you by your born-again spirit. They that are "led by the spirit" are the mature of God (according to Romans 8:14). You're not just a child of God. Rather, you are the mature of the Lord. You know God's ways. When a person is a child they are learning their parents' ways. They are learning what the parents will accept and what they will not accept. They are learning how far they can go. They are learning how many times to ask or when they need to shut up. They learn when their parents are serious. They learn if this is a good time to try it again. After a while of growing up, they begin to discern their parents' ways and they don't necessarily have to ask. They say, "No. Mama or Daddy wouldn't like that. I think they may like that." "What am I going to get them for Christmas? I think they may like that." "That looks like something Daddy might like." "Oh yea, that's Mama's favorite color." You start to discern things without having to ask all of the time. Psalm 16:8 continues to say,

---

8. I have set the Lord always before me: because he is at my right hand, I shall not be moved.

9. Therefore my heart is glad, and my glory rejoiceth: my flesh also shall rest in hope.

This is when you have the "peace that passes understanding." Situations may happen in life, such as unplanned circumstances, yet, you are still holding your peace, because you know that God has it in control. You know that God is greater than anybody, anytime, or any situation. You're walking with Him. He's your God. He's your Heavenly Father. He says, "I love them that love me, and they that seek me early shall find me" (Proverbs 8:17).

You can still be confident. You're "righteous and bold as a lion", according to Proverbs 28:1. You're not all beat down by the situation. People may come against you with a situation. Yet, you are still calm, cool, collected, and confident. They are expecting you to be distraught. Yet, you're walking with your head up. You're calm, well-balanced, and stable. The sheer confidence of your manner will cause your adversary to become *discombobulated*. Because, they expected you to act one way, yet, you are acting another way. You're calm, cool, collected, and confident. That is resistance. That's peaceful resistance. The Bible says, "Submit yourself unto God. Resist the devil and he will flee from you" (James 4:7). Why? It's because, you're starting to look like God. You've been spending so much time with God that you're starting to look like Him. Jesus is the Lion of Judah. You're a lamb that's starting to look like a Lion. You're a lamb that looks like a lion. You've been spending so much time with God that you're starting to look like Him! Psalm 16:9 goes on to say,

> 9. Therefore my heart is glad, and my glory rejoiceth: my flesh also shall rest in hope.

Your "glory" is your "boldness and confidence." You're calm, cool, collected, and well-balanced. You know "God's got this!" And, "I'm in God." "We're all good."

---

10. For thou wilt not leave my soul in hell; neither wilt thou suffer thine Holy One to see corruption.

So, no matter what "hell" you're going through in life. No matter what "hell" you're going through on your job. No matter what "hell" you're going through in your finances. No matter what "hell" you're going through from the doctor's report. No matter what "hell" the family is reporting. No matter what "hell" is going on in your neighborhood. No matter what "hell" is going on in your nation. You have to focus on what God says.

10. For thou wilt not leave my soul in hell; neither wilt thou suffer thine Holy One to see corruption.

11. Thou wilt shew me the path of life: in thy presence is fullness of joy; at thy right hand there are pleasures for evermore.

God says, He's going to show you the path out of this into a better day, into a brighter day, into a higher day, and into the favor of God. So, you can say, "I'm just going to keep on seeking you each and every day Lord. Which has been my routine. I'm just going to keep on seeking you early."

For example, Daniel's enemies came against him and they said they were going to cast him into the lion's den if he kept on praying to God. Daniel opened his window and started praying even louder unto his God three times a day. He wasn't going to let them intimidate him. He was cast into the lion's den. Yet, God shut the mouth of the lions. The king was amazed and turned his heart to Daniel's God. Then, Daniel's enemies were thrown into the lion's den and they were devoured. Then, the laws of the whole nation were changed to reverence Daniel's God, because of his boldness. Psalm 16:11 continues to say,

---

11. Thou wilt shew me the path of life: in thy presence is fullness of joy; at thy right hand, there are pleasures for evermore.

Now let's look back at Proverbs 8: 17-21.

> 17. I love them that love me; and those that seek me early shall find me.
>
> 18. Riches and honour are with me; yea, durable riches and righteousness.
>
> 19. My fruit is better than gold, yea, than fine gold; and my revenue than choice silver.
>
> 20. I lead in the way of righteousness, in the midst of the paths of judgment:
>
> 21. That I may cause those that love me to inherit substance; and I will fill their treasures.

The "fruit" of your relationship with God is "better than gold." The outgrowth of you loving Him and spending time with Him is "better than gold." God says, "Not only am I going to make you rich in the area of finances, but I'm going to make you truly wealthy." To be wealthy means having more than money. To be truly wealthy is to be healthy, whole, well, sound, safe, and secure. It's having fullness of life. Again, Proverbs 8:17-21 says,

17. I love them that love me; and those that seek me early shall find me.

18. Riches and honour are with me; yea, durable riches and righteousness.

19. My fruit is better than gold, yea, than fine gold; and my revenue than choice silver.

20. I lead in the way of righteousness, in the midst of the paths of judgment:

21. That I may cause those that love me to inherit substance; and I will fill their treasures.

You are now in the process of becoming rich. God is causing you to inherit substance. God is filling your "treasures." We know that "treasures" are bank accounts, savings accounts, investment accounts, and other forms of storehouses or investments. God promises those who love Him that He will love them in a special way. Now, we know that God loves everybody. However, He's talking about a special love, affection, and allegiance that He has for the people who have a special love, affection, and allegiance for Him. Your allegiance to God will be shown through your behavior. It will be shown in your lifestyle. It will be shown in your devotion to God's principles. God loves people who are committed to living by His principles in the earth. It's one thing to say that you love God, however, if you don't do what He said to do, then, those are fruitless, futile, and useless words. There are many people who say that they love God, but they do not demonstrate His nature. For example, the United States is often called a Christian nation. If you ask someone if they are a Christian, then, they will say, "Oh, Yes. I'm a Christian. I was born into a Christian family. We were raised up in church. We're a Christian family." Yet, if you looked at their lifestyle, then, you wouldn't know it. Why? It's because they are not committed to living by God's principles. They are "Christian" in name only. They are "Christian" in religion. Like it's said that the United States is a "Christian Nation." That's the "banner" over the nation. However, if you looked at many aspects of the nations' history, then, you wouldn't see the nature of Jesus Christ or of the Spirit of God. You won't receive the blessings of being a true Christian if you're not living a Christian lifestyle. You can say that you are a Christian, but, if you haven't received Jesus Christ as Lord and Savior, then, you're not saved. If you're not obeying His principles, then, you're not blessed. So, you can say that you're a part of a Christian nation, and that you're a part of a Christian family, and that you're a part of the Christian religion, yet, if you haven't accepted Jesus Christ as Lord and Savior by repenting of your sins and asking Him to come into your heart, and are living a life devoted to Him, then, you're not saved. And, if you're not saved and you're not obeying His principles in your lifestyle, then, you're not blessed. Proverbs 8:18 says, "Riches and honor are with me; yes, durable riches and righteousness." God is saying that those who seek His principles and wisdom, will also find "riches and honor; yes, durable riches and righteousness." In other words, the result of actually discovering God's principles for living will also reveal to you keys to becoming financially free. That's God's will. It's a good thing! It's a good thing to be free from poverty. It's a good thing to have more than enough. It's a good thing to have abundance and success on your job, success in your businesses, success in your investments, success in your home, success in your family, success in school, success in college, etc. It's good. It's acceptable. It's God's desire. 3 John 2 says, "Beloved, I wish (or desire) above all things that you prosper and be in health, even as your soul prospers." God also says in Psalm 35:27,

---

27. Let them shout for joy, and be glad, that favour my righteous cause: yea, let them say continually, Let the Lord be magnified, which hath pleasure in the prosperity of his servant.

God has pleasure in our prosperity. God delights in our being blessed. He delights in us having blessing and favor and things going well with us. God is good. He loves us. He loves His children. Jesus says in John 10:10,

10. The thief cometh not, but for to steal, and to kill, and to destroy: I am come that they might have life, and that they might have it more abundantly.

God says in 1 Timothy 6:17,

17. Charge them that are rich in this world, that they be not highminded, nor trust in uncertain riches, but in the living God, who giveth us richly all things to enjoy.

God wants to see you blessed. God's principles will make you financially free as you study them and follow after Him. God wants you to be financially free. God wants you to obtain "riches and honor." God has principles in His word that encourages us toward diligent pursuits of our gifts and talents that He has put inside of us. He encourages us to use the intelligence He has given us to actively pursue the attainment of wealth. That's His desire. That's His will. You need to know this. You need to teach your children this. You need to encourage your family toward this. You need to encourage other saints towards this. It's not His will for you to be poor. It's not His will for you to be defeated. It's not His will for you to not have enough. It's not acceptable. So, don't accept it. It's not something you should get accustomed to. You may be in a situation where you don't have enough now, or, you may be in a situation where you have lived with not enough, but, God says, it's His desire for you to have more than enough. He wants your blessing to come to you. He wants you to have everything that Jesus died on the cross for you to have. He is your redeemer. He is your restorer. Amen. Hallelujah!

It is wisdom to obey God's admonitions to us to study and pursue the knowledge necessary to become financially free. God has admonitions in the Bible that tell us to study. God "wishes above all things that you prosper, and be in health, even as your soul prospers" (according to 3 John 2). He tells you to "get wisdom, get understanding" (Proverbs 4:7). He didn't say that "understanding" would just drop down on you like rain. Rather, He's instructing you to pursue understanding. It is wisdom to obey God's admonitions to study and pursue the knowledge necessary to become financially free. It is not enough to have a moral life. No. It is through having a *diligent* life that is focused on your unique gifts and talents that you will become financially free. It's through getting the knowledge that is aligned with your natural gifts, talents, time, skill, knowledge, opportunities, family, etc., that will give you, your children, and your family an advantage. God wants you to be righteous and *rich*. That's His desire. There have been many business people who followed after Christian business and financial principles of diligence. They started their businesses and industries and became rich, wealthy, and well known. There are many well-known companies with over 100 years in business in the United States that were started by Christian business people. They were righteous and they became rich. They believed God to have possession of what God desired for them in the earth, and not just to be moral or righteous. You should believe God to have everything that He has for you to have in life. You can accomplish more for God if you have more financial and material resources. This truly is a key for you to "GAIN 20/20 VISION FOR THE NEW DECADE". In most cases, this is not taught in church, school, or most homes. Many Christians go for years and years living a righteous life of worshipping God, but they also need to be admonished to take possession of the financial and material blessing that God desires for them to have. For example, Christians should be encouraged to start that class, or to get that degree, take that course or start selling real estate, etc. Do something to advance yourself so that you can get more out of life than what you're getting now. It's not just through your prayer. Your prayer can heal your body. Your prayer can deliver your children out of a desperate situation. Your prayer can bring favor for your situation financially and give you opportunities, but in order for you to have a continual flow of provision and advantage, then, you must do more in order to possess more. Through our relationship with God we will gain insights as to how to pursue successful living. Specific evidence of a successful life, according to Proverbs 8:18 are "Riches and honor" and "durable riches and righteousness". In other words, the sign that you have discovered all of God's keys for having a successful life will also be a financially wealthy life. The sign that you have gotten everything that God desires for you to obtain from walking with Him in life will be that you also gain a wealthy life before your life ends. Along the journey, you should have accumulated wisdom, righteousness, and wealth. That's God's will for your life. In order for you to obtain this condition in your life, you must first accept it in your heart as truly God's desire for your life. You have to make room for riches in your heart. You have to believe that it's the will of God for you to be satisfied with health, wealth, happiness, peace, success, favor, and blessing on your family. You must believe that whatever you set your hands to will prosper. You must believe that wherever you set your feet He's given it to you to have dominion. You should make room for the Blessing in your life by making room for the Blessing in your heart first. The Blessing is your birthright. If you make room for it in your heart, then, you can make room for it in your life. That can help you start moving towards it. You can believe for it. If you believe that it's possible, then, you can have it.

Shattered By A Higher Vision

For example, NASA declared the vision of going to the Moon. They placed an image of the Moon on the wall. Everybody walking around the office at NASA saw the picture of the Moon. Everybody was talking about "the Moon, the Moon, the Moon." It seemed impossible. It didn't make sense to the normal, limited mind. "The Moon. The Moon. The Moon" was the vision. You walked in the office in the morning and the janitor was talking about "the Moon, the Moon, the Moon . . ." Everybody was talking about the Moon, until eventually the first man walked on the Moon. NASA sent a man to the Moon! It seemed impossible. Yet, the vision broke out of the Earth's atmosphere. The vision broke out of the Earth limitations. It broke out of what was normal. It broke out of what was natural. The natural limits were shattered by a higher vision of what was desired. The higher vision was obtained. The words of this book are a higher vision for you, your family, your children, and future generations. This Word is given for you to *"break out!"* No matter what your past may have been. No matter what the gravitational pull of your past may be, you can break out to a higher future. Proverbs 4:7 says,

7. Wisdom is the principal thing;
therefore get wisdom: and with all
thy getting get understanding.

Wealth Is The Fruit of Godly Living

Proverbs 8: 19-21 clearly shows us the results God desires for those in relationship with Him:

19. My fruit is better than gold, yes, than fine gold; and my revenue than choice silver.

20. I lead in the way of righteousness, in the midst of the paths of judgment:

21. That I may cause those that love me to inherit substance; and I will fill their treasures.

"Fruit" is the outgrowth of a "seed". Jesus said in the parable of the "Sower" in Mark 4:1-20, "the sower sows the Word." The "seed" is the Word of God. You are "good ground". Jesus talked about different types of ground. He talked about "wayside". He talked about "stony ground". He talked about "thorny ground". And, He talked about "good ground." Then, He talked about three levels of output from the "good ground." He talked about "thirtyfold, sixtyfold, and one-hundredfold." It's your responsibility as being the "hearer" of the Word to determine what kind of ground you are. Jesus said, "He that has ears to hear, let him hear." So, it's your responsibility to determine what kind of ground you are. The seed is good. The sower is good. The seed knows what to do. The sower is doing what he's supposed to do. Yet, it's up to you as to what kind of ground you are and what kind of harvest you will gain. You determine if you will gain a harvest at all and at what level. Proverbs 8:19-21 says,

> 19. My fruit is better than gold, yes, than fine gold; and my revenue than choice silver.

> 20. I lead in the way of righteousness, in the midst of the paths of judgment:
>
> 21. That I may cause those that love me to inherit substance; and I will fill their treasures.

God is speaking in financial terms. He says, "gold", "fine gold", and "revenue." That's money. You don't have to be a financial genius to know that if God is talking to you about "gold", "fine gold", and "revenue" and "silver", then, He is talking about business, economics, and money. However, God is also talking about "fruit." He says, "My fruit is better than gold, yes, than fine gold; and my revenue than choice silver." He is saying, "As a result of you spending time with me, loving me, and walking with me in your lifestyle, not only will you become financially rich, but you will become *enriched*." You will become a wealthier person. Not only from the finances that you will gain in your bank accounts or investments, but you yourself will become enriched. You will think wealthy thoughts. You will feel that you're sufficient for whatever situation or circumstance that you come in contact with.

You will be like the Apostle Paul who says, "I can do all things through Christ which strengthens me." He didn't say, "Jesus can do all things." He said, "*I can* do all things through Christ which strengthens me." He says, "I'm involved. I'm going to do the things!" He says, "I can do all things through Christ which strengthens me." In other words, "It's through my relationship with Christ. Yet, it will be me that actually physically does it. I'm going to get it done." He said, "No matter what I'm facing. None of these things move me, neither count I my life dear unto myself, so that I may finish my course with joy and the ministry that I have received from the Lord Jesus Christ" (Acts 20:24) Why? It's because the Apostle Paul was enriched by his relationship with the Lord Jesus Christ. So, the "fruit" of that relationship was great boldness and great confidence in his own capability to "do all things through Christ" which strengthened him to do it. No matter what it was. He said, "And none of these things move me". God didn't say that you wouldn't be faced with "things." Yet, you can say like the Apostle Paul, "None of these things move me." We have been "called, justified, and glorified" (according to Romans 8:30). It goes on to say in Romans 8:31-34

31. What shall we then say to these things? If God be for us, who can be against us?

32. He that spared not his own Son, but delivered him up for us all, how shall he not with him also freely give us all things?

33. Who shall lay any thing to the charge of God's elect? It is God that justifieth.

34. Who is he that condemneth? It is Christ that died, yea rather, that is risen again, who is even at the right hand of God, who also maketh intercession for us.

So, you're feeling sufficient, because the outgrowth of the seed of God's Word that has been planted in the "good ground" of your heart is that you have been "enriched". You have been "emboldened." You have been enriched by the presence of God so that you can feel sufficient. So, not only do you have the finances, but you also have become wealthy. You *are* wealth. The finances on the outside are just a reflection of the fact that you have become enriched on the inside from truly getting to know God.

You know that "My God shall supply all of my needs according to His riches in glory by Christ Jesus" (Philippians 4:19). You're not limited by what's in the world or the world system. You're not limited by what they say on your job. You're not limited by what they say about the economy. You're not limited by what they say is available. Rather, you say, "My God shall supply all of my needs according to His riches in glory by Christ Jesus" (Philippians 4:19). The scripture says, "My God . . ." In other words, you know Him personally. You've been walking with Him. You have been enriched. Not only do you have riches, rather, you have been enriched. And, when you're enriched, then, there is nothing that anyone can take from you. They can try to take or disturb, or threaten the things on the outside, but they can't take what's on the inside. If they try to take it from you, then, you can make it back by the next year. It's because you have been enriched with the wisdom of how to obtain wealth. Godly wisdom to get wealth comes from God. He is the source of wealth and riches. For example, it's been said that if all of the money were taking from the wealthiest people in the world and distributed to everyone else, then, they would have it all back in a short period of time. It's said that the top 1-3% of people on Earth, particularly in the United States, own and control more than 90% of the wealth on Earth. So, the wealth is controlled by a very small percentage of people on the planet. Some people say, "That's not fair!" They say, "They need to take that money from them and spread it around to everybody on the planet, so that there would be more equity in the economy on Earth." Contrarily, it's been said, "If you took the wealth from those that have it and who had the wisdom to gain it, and, if you spread it to everyone on the Earth, then, it would be right back in the same hands that had it before within a short period of time." Why? It's because the ones that had it have been enriched with the mindset of wealth. They know how to get it. They know the thinking process. They know the mindset. They know how to manage it. They know how to *draw* it to themselves with their actions and activities. So, the money would be right back in the same hands, unless those who don't currently have money takes time to gain the same wisdom, understanding, and knowledge that the ones that have it has. The only way that you will get your portion and share is if you get the same wisdom, understanding, and knowledge that the wealthy has, and apply the same diligence. Then, you will get your portion and your share in this life. Therefore, it is critical that you "GAIN 20/20 VISION FOR THE NEW DECADE! A Step By Step Path To A More Successful Future."

God Can Reveal Secrets To You

God can reveal secrets, insights, and wisdom to you. He may say, "Go read that book." Or, He may say, "Go take that class". Or, He may say, "Go look that information up now". He can strengthen you in your diligence, so that you can say, "I can do all things through Christ which strengthens me." Proverbs 8:20 says,

20. I lead in the way of righteousness, in the midst of the paths of judgment.

21. That I may cause those that love me to inherit substance: and I will fill their treasures.

God says, "I'm leading you in the paths of righteousness, so that I may cause you to inherit substance (or wealth)." In other words, it will start to come to you, because you have positioned yourself and you have conditioned yourself, and you are engaged in the activities that cause prosperous things to come to you. It's because you're doing the things that make good things come your way. It's because you have been fellowshipping with God. You're in the right place, at the right time, doing the right things, and interacting with the right people. God can bring the right people. People that you never knew that you would get in contact with. You will come into contact with them at the right time. He will "fill our treasures." You should have expectation of your bank accounts and treasures being filled as you seek the Lord. That is His promise to you. That's the Word of the Lord for you for the new decade. From all of your tithes and offerings and all of your faithfulness in giving and living, then, God says, "There's a *laid up* inheritance for you." These verses reveal to us God's will regarding our relationship with Him. He desires that in our relationship with Him we will develop the wisdom necessary to obtain "riches and honor." It's not just for you to feel good. Yet, spending time with the Lord will make you feel better. He will give you peace, healing, comfort, etc. The Holy Spirit is the

Comforter. Furthermore, the Holy Spirit is the Counselor. If you listen to Him, then, He will give you direction. He will direct you to do something. He will direct you to go somewhere. He will direct you to "take that class." He will direct you to "read that book." He will direct you to "start that business." He will direct you to "Get wisdom; and with all your getting, get understanding" (Proverbs 4:7). The Holy Spirit will say, according to Ecclesiastes 7:11-12,

> 11. Wisdom is good with an inheritance: and by it there is profit to them that see the sun.
>
> 12. For wisdom is a defence, and money is a defence: but the excellency of knowledge is, that wisdom giveth life to them that have it.

Therefore, He's telling you to "get wisdom" and "understanding", because there is "profit" available to you through gaining wisdom and understanding. He wants to lead you to a place where you and your family will obtain "durable riches and righteousness", such as houses, land, businesses, industry, oil, gold, silver, technology, media, manufacturing, etc. Make room for this in your heart. Make room for this for your family. If you will make room for this in your heart, then, you are also spiritually making room for it in your family in the current generation and for future generations. If you will let the seed be planted in your heart, then, you are making room for it in your family. The "Seed" is the Word of God. The "sower soweth the Word." You are the "good ground" (Mark 4:14-20). Proverbs 8:19 says,

> 19. My fruit is better than gold, yea, than fine gold; and my revenue than choice silver.

So, if you make room for it in your heart, then, you are making room for it in your family. You're making room for it in your future generations. You're making room for it in your finances. You're making room for it in your reality. You're making room for it in your community. You're making room for it in your city. You're making room for it in your nation. You're making room for it in the Body of Christ. You're making room for it by your faith and believing in and accepting the Word of God. It's a Seed. It's a vision. You're letting the will of God be planted in your spirit, and then, the Holy Spirit can let the Word *run swiftly* throughout the Earth and manifest and you will see a higher rise. Arise! Arise! Arise! Arise in your life. Arise in your family's life. Arise in future generations. God wants the summation of your life to be filled with much substance. God wants the summation of you walking with Him, fellowshipping with Him, knowing Him, being in covenant with Him, being His child, and being in love with Him to be filled with much substance. He promises that if you will follow His principles, His wisdom will lead you to full bank accounts and investments, according to Proverbs 8:21, which says,

21. That I may cause those that love me to inherit substance; and I will fill their treasures.

That is God's will. I decree, according to Deuteronomy 16:15b (NIV),

15b. . . . For the Lord your God will bless you in all your harvest and in all the work of your hands, and your joy will be complete.

This is a key to help you "GAIN 20/20 VISION FOR THE NEW DECADE! A Step By Step Path To A More Successful Future." We've been looking at key 4) "Finances."

CHAPTER SEVEN

Peace of Mind: The 5th Essential Key To A More Successful New Decade

In this book, "GAIN 20/20 VISION FOR THE NEW DECADE! A Step By Step Path To A More Successful Future" I have talked to you about the first four essential keys to gaining the proper vision for success in this new decade and beyond. I have talked to you about key 1) "God." The beginning place for success is our relationship with God. 2) "Marriage & Family." The next closest relationship is with our marriage and family. The husband and wife relationship is critical, because the "two becomes one." Therefore, learning how to have peace and respect in that relationship is a critical key to overall success in life. Also, it's key that the children learn to honor and respect their parents. Our relationship with brothers, sisters, aunts, uncles, cousins, and others outside of our family is key to success in our overall life. 3) "Health." Good health is essential to our total success. Many times our relationship with God, family, and others greatly impacts the quality of our health. 4) "Finances." Your relationship with God through living according to His Word and exercising diligence in the use of your gifts and talents is key to your financial success. As you seek God for wisdom and insight, then, He will bless your finances.

We all want peace of mind.

Now, finally in this book "GAIN 20/20 VISION FOR THE NEW DECADE!" I want to talk to you about a desire that we all have after all has been said and done and nothing else can be said and done. The desire is for key number 5) "Peace of Mind." We all want peace of mind. We all need peace of mind. That is a key to prosperity. You can have financial prosperity. Yet, if you don't have peace of mind, then, you can't enjoy it. If you're always looking over your shoulder, then, you can't enjoy it. Or, if you're always concerned about your health, then, you can't fully even enjoy your financial prosperity. Or, if you don't have peace in your relationships, then, your overall enjoyment of life is diminished. As we mentioned earlier, one of the greatest sources of challenge for our health is in our relationships with others. If you can have peace with yourself and peace with others, then, you will have peace of mind. If you know who you are, love yourself, appreciate yourself, and accept yourself, then, you will have peace with yourself. The Bible says in Ephesians 5:29, "For no man ever yet hated his own flesh; but nourisheth and cherisheth it, even as the Lord the church." The normal person will make sure that if no one else eats, then, certainly, he or she will eat. You make sure that you get some rest. If you're cold, then, you make sure that you have on a coat or warm sweater to get warm. You will make sure that you don't have to walk, but that you have gas in your car. You will make sure that you're comfortable. If it's hot, then, you will make sure that you have a fan on you or have on the air conditioner. Why? It's because, you're "nourishing and cherishing" yourself, because you love yourself. Every person in a normal state of mind loves him or herself. The scripture goes on to say that as a husband loves himself, then, he should love his wife in that same way. How he loves his wife is a reflection of how he first loves himself. This is a normal state. Therefore, if you can have peace with yourself and peace with others, then, you can have peace of mind. Peace with yourself starts with your relationship with God. When you have that "Blessed assurance, Jesus is mine, O' what a foretaste of glory divine, heir of salvation, purchase of love, born of His Spirit, washed in His blood, This is my story, this is my song, praising my Savior, all the day long." When you have peace with God, then, you will have peace of mind. When you have peace with God, then, you are confident that if you were to close your eyes for the last time tonight, then, you have the blessed assurance that the next time that you opened your eyes you would be in Heaven in the presence of the Lord Jesus Christ. Peace of mind comes from your knowing that "My God shall supply all my need, according to His riches in glory, by

Christ Jesus" (Philippians 4:19). In the midst of famine, need, trouble, turmoil, pestilences, disease, and viruses in the world, then, you have the confidence of Psalm 91, which says:

---

1. He that dwelleth in the secret place of the most High shall abide under the shadow of the Almighty.

2. I will say of the Lord, He is my refuge and my fortress: my God; in him will I trust.

3. Surely he shall deliver thee from the snare of the fowler, and from the noisome pestilence.

4. He shall cover thee with his feathers, and under his wings shalt thou trust: his truth shall be they shield and buckler.

5. Thou shalt not be afraid for the terror by night; nor for the arrow that flieth by day;

6. Nor for the pestilence that walketh in darkness; nor for the destruction that wasteth at noon day.

7. A thousand shall fall at thy side, and ten thousand at thy right hand; but it shall not come nigh thee.

8. Only with thine eyes shalt thou behold and see the reward of the wicked.

9. Because thou hast made the Lord, which is my refuge, even the most High, thy habitation;

10. There shall no evil befall thee, neither shall any plague come nigh thy dwelling.

11. For he shall give his angels charge over thee, to keep thee in all thy ways.

12. They shall bear thee up in their hands, lest thou dash thy foot against a stone.

13. Thou shalt tread upon the lion and adder: the young lion and the dragon shalt thou trample under feet.

14. Because he hath set his love upon me, therefore will I deliver him: I will set him on high, because he hath known my name.

15. He shall call upon me, and I will answer him: I will be with him in trouble; I will deliver him, and honour him.

16. With long life will I satisfy him, and shew him my salvation.

This is that peace that you have, because of your relationship with God. Knowing Who God is, and knowing His will for your life is the key to peace of mind. We know it's God's will for us to have peace with other people.

Control Yourself For Peace of Mind

Proverbs 15:1 gives us an answer to maintaining peace with people. It says, "A soft answer turns away wrath: but grievous words stir up anger." This also helps us to maintain peace with ourselves, and with God. Sometimes you have to subdue your feelings and responses in order to maintain peace. Some things you have to do "for peace sake." There are a lot of things that people can take from you, but, don't let them take your peace. Jesus told his disciples "In your patience possess ye your souls" (Luke 21:19). In other words, you keep possession of your soul. You keep possession of your mind. You keep possession of your will. You keep possession of your emotions. You keep possession of your feelings. In your patience you will keep possession of your soul. That patience is self-control. This is a key to peace. In your longsuffering you keep possession of your soul. You stay self-possessed. Don't let anyone take your soul. Don't let anyone make you mad. Don't let anyone make you angry. Don't let anyone make you afraid. Don't let anyone make you lose control. No. You stay self-possessed. You take possession of your own soul. You keep possession of your soul. You keep possession of your feelings. You keep possession of your joy. Don't let anyone take your joy. The devil tries to steal your joy. But, the "joy of the Lord is your strength." If you let the devil and people's attitudes steal your joy, then, you will lose your strength. You will lose your ability to be vibrant and effective in life if you let the devil steal you joy. You can feel a little frustrated with people, or situations and circumstances, such as the traffic or the bills and talking on the phone with bill collectors, or a delay in your schedule, but you can still be joyful, by knowing that "My God shall supply all my needs, according to His riches in glory by Christ Jesus"(Philippians 4:19). God has the whole world in His hands. The earth is the Lord's and the fullness thereof, the world and they that dwell therein (Psalm 24:1). We are His people and the sheep of His pasture (Psalm 100:3). God controls it all and you're in God's hand, and you have peace with God. Jesus said, "Peace I leave with you. My peace give I unto you. Not as the world giveth, give I unto you. Let not your heart be trouble, neither let it be afraid" (John 14:27). Now, Jesus said, "Let not your heart be troubled . . ." That tells me that I have power to "let it" or to not "let it." That tells me that I'm in control. That tells me that I'm not being pulled around and whipped around by life like a kite tail. Out of control. In other words, "Don't let the tail wag the dog." The "dog" should "wag" his own "tail." Don't let life "wag" you. Rather, you keep control of life and how you're going to walk through life. Jesus said, "In your patience possess you your souls" (Luke 21:19). Sometimes people can be difficult. Sometimes we can come in contact with difficult personalities. Some people can be more irritating than others. Some people can be instigating. We all have different personalities. You don't have to let anyone "get on your nerves." Don't let anyone "get on your last nerve." You need to keep your nerves self-possessed. Put on the whole armor of God so that they can't get to your nerves. Put on the "helmet of salvation", "the breastplate of righteousness", and "your feet shod with the preparation of the gospel of peace." We have peace with God. Don't let anyone take your peace. People shouldn't be able to get to your "last nerve." You should keep on the whole armor of God to protect your nerves.

Tools For Self-Control

In Psalm 119:164-165 the Bible gives you an answer for maintaining peace of mind.

> 164. Seven times a day do I praise thee because of thy righteous judgments.

> 165. Great peace have they which
> love thy law: and nothing shall offend
> them.

This scripture will help you "GAIN 20/20 VISION FOR THE NEW DECADE!" If you're living a life where you're worshipping and praising God through singing, and you're being thankful throughout the day, then, you will have more peace. As you say to the Lord, "Thank you Lord that I woke up this morning in my right mind. I can get out of the bed on my own two feet. I can hear. I can see. I can stretch out my limbs. I can take a shower. Thank you Lord. I can brush my teeth. I can go to the refrigerator and get some water or orange juice. I have shelter. I can put on some clothes. Thank you Lord that my brain can process information. Thank for all the good things you've given me." Then, throughout the day you keep on thanking and praising God by saying, "Thank you Lord for making a way on that situation. Thank you for helping me pay my bills. Thank you for helping me in that conversation..." "Seven times a day do I praise thee because of thy righteous judgments" (Psalm 119:164). "Seven" is the perfect number. In other words, King David was saying that he lived a lifestyle of continual praise. He lived a life of continual fellowship with God by giving Him continual thanksgiving. By having this lifestyle of continual praise it builds up your joy. The joy of the Lord is your strength. This helps you to stay in a state of peace of mind. As you maintain your joy level, then, your joy becomes a "defense against offence." It prevents people from getting on your last nerve. It creates a "force-field" around your inner sanctum. The "force-field" of joy surrounds your heart and soul. It increases your strength of temperance, which is a fruit of the spirit. Jesus said, "In your patience possess you your souls" (Luke 21:19). Your self-control or temperance is a key to protecting your soul. "Temperance" is a fruit of the spirit, "against such there is no law." There is no power that can penetrate your force field, if you maintain the fruit of the spirit. Your heart is full of the fruit of the spirit, which is love (perfect love casts out fear. So, you're not afraid.) Joy (the joy of the Lord is your strength). Peace (peace, which passes understanding. Even if you don't understand it you're not stress out. You're not confused, because you have peace, which passes understanding). Longsuffering, (you have patience, which possesses your soul). Goodness, (you treat people with goodness). Gentleness, (you treat people in a gentle way). Meekness, (you're not all rough and puffed up, but you have a mildness in how you treat others). Faith, (you operate in the spirit of faith and courage in how you take on life). Temperance, (which is self-control). Against such there is no law."

Psalm 119:164-165 says,

---

164. Seven times a day do I praise thee because of thy righteous judgments.

165. Great peace have they which love thy law: and nothing shall offend them.

"Great peace" is gained from reading three or more chapters of the Bible everyday, so as to build a fence or wall around your soul in order to protect your heart from being offended or made afraid. You should build up your heart against the stresses and assaults of life. Psalm 91:5-12 promises you protection and insulation from the assaults of life. This is what it says,

5. Thou shalt not be afraid for the terror by night; nor for the arrow that flieth by day;

6. Nor for the pestilence that walketh in darkness; nor for the destruction that wasteth at noonday.

7. A thousand shall fall at thy side, and ten thousand at thy right hand; but it shall not come nigh thee.

8. Only with thine eyes shalt thou behold and see the reward of the wicked.

9. Because thou hast made the Lord, which is my refuge, even the most High, thy habitation;

10. There shall no evil befall thee, neither shall any plague come nigh they dwelling.

11. For he shall give his angels charge over thee, to keep thee in all thy ways.

> 12. They shall bear thee up in their hands, lest thou dash thy foot against a stone.

So, you can have peace of mind in dealing with people, circumstances, and the events of the world. Psalm 119:164-165 says,

> 164. Seven times a day do I praise thee because of thy righteous judgments.
>
> 165. Great peace have they which love thy law: and nothing shall offend them.

You build a "fence against offence." You build a wall around your heart and mind by putting on the whole armor of God. Ephesians 6:10-18 has this to say about the whole armor of God:

10. Finally, my brethren, be strong in the Lord, and in the power of his might.

11. Put on the whole armour of God, that ye may be able to stand against the wiles of the devil.

12. For we wrestle not against flesh and blood, but against principalities, against powers, against the rulers of the darkness of this world, against spiritual wickedness in high places.

13. Wherefore take unto you the whole armour of God, that ye may be able to withstand in the evil day, and having done all, to stand.

14. Stand therefore, having your loins girt about with truth, and having on the the breastplate of righteousness;

15. And your feet shod with the preparation of the gospel of peace;

16. Above all taking the shield of faith, wherewith ye shall be able to quench all the fiery darts of the wicked.

17. And take the helmet of salvation, and the sword of the Spirit, which is the word of God:

18. Praying always with all prayer and supplication in the Spirit, and watching thereunto with all perseverance and supplication for all saints.

This is how you "GAIN 20/20 VISION FOR THE NEW DECADE!" You have to be equipped for success.

The Right Answer For Peace

Sometimes silence is the softest answer. When someone is trying to instigate an argument or baiting you into conflict, then, sometime the softest answer is silence. Proverbs 15:1 says,

1. A soft answer turns away wrath:
but grievous words stir up anger.

You often have to be cautious in how you answer some people. Or, when someone says something that is close to getting on your last nerve by trying to work through your armor to get to your soul, then, that's when you have to "in your patience possess you your soul" (Luke 21:19). Keep possession of your soul. Keep possession of your mind, your will, your emotions, your personality, your disposition, and your intellect. You should keep possession of that. Don't let anyone make you mad. Don't let anyone make you afraid. Don't let anyone make you hysterical. Don't let anyone make you depressed. Don't let anyone make you feel bad. Don't let anyone make you feel intimidated. Don't let anyone make you feel of low self-esteem or feel unqualified. No. Rather, "in your patience possess you your soul" (Luke 21:19). Keep self-possession of your mind, your will, your emotions, your personality, your disposition, your intellect, your self-value, your self-esteem, and your self-confidence. And, sometimes silence is the softest answer. When someone is trying to bait you or draw you into a situation or conversation or say something to slight you to make you feel bad or make you feel less than because they want to cut you, then, don't let them get to your last nerve. Keep on the whole armor of God. And, "in your patience possess you your soul." A soft answer will turn away your wrath and it will turn away their wrath, but grievous words stir up anger in the situation. It's been said, "Sometimes you have to bite your tongue." Well, you don't necessarily have to bite your tongue, but you can hold your answer in. Then, maintain the peace that you have within. Jesus said, "Peace I leave with you. My peace I give unto you. Not as the world giveth, give I unto you. Let not your heart be troubled, neither let it be afraid" (John 14:27). You have the power to "let" it or to "not let" it. You have the power to "allow it" or to "not allow it." In others words, you're in control of your own mind. You're in control of your own emotions. You're in control of your own feelings. No one can make you feel bad or make you feel less or make you feel out of your mind with anger or fear, etc. You can control it. You can subdue it. How? With the "truth." You can subdue it with the "helmet of salvation" ("For I am not ashamed of the Gospel of Jesus Christ, for it is the power of God unto salvation to everyone that believeth; to the Jew first and also to the Greek, for therein is the righteousness of God revealed from faith to faith. As it is written, The just shall live by faith" Romans 1:16-17). You can subdue it with the "breastplate of righteousness" ("For He hath made Him to be sin for us Who know no sin, that we might be made the righteousness of God in Him" 2 Corinthians 5:21). "The wicked flee when no man pursues, but the righteous is bold as a lion" (Proverbs 28:1). You are righteous! You must keep your "loins girt about with truth". Jesus said, "I am the way, the truth, and the life. No man cometh unto the Father, but by me" (John 14:6). "Thy word is truth" (John 17:17). "Whatsoever things are true, whatsoever things are honest, whatsoever things are just, whatsoever things are pure, whatsoever things are lovely, whatsoever things are of good report. If there be any virtue and if there be any praise, think on these things" (Philippians 4:8-9). You have the power to choose your own feelings and response to life's situations. Regarding avoiding conflict with people, one of the wisest things that we can do is control ourselves, and our mouths. No one controls your mouth, but you. No one can make you say something. No one can make you burst out with wrath or anger. No one can make you respond to something. When Jesus stood before the governor and the scribes and Pharisees were accusing Him, he didn't say anything. He kept his mouth closed. The governor marveled. Jesus had self-control. No one controls your mouth but you. Matthew 27:11-14 gives the story,

11. And Jesus stood before the governor: and the governor asked him, saying, Art thou the King of the Jews? And Jesus said unto him, Thou sayest,

12. And when he was accused of the chief priests and elders, he answered nothing.

13. Then said Pilate unto him, Hearest thou not how many things they witness against thee?

14. And he answered him to never a word; insomuch that the governor marvelled greatly.

You can't control what other people say or do. However, you can control how you respond. And, often, how you respond will determine whether the conflict escalates or de-escalates. This truly is a powerful key to maintaining peace of mind. Most of the times we can maintain peace with ourselves, particularly, if we have established peace with God through obeying His Word. For example, if you're at home by yourself, you generally can maintain peace of mind. However, it's unpredictable how people will respond in life. Sometimes you don't know how people will respond from one day to another. God is stable. God's Word is stable. God's principles are stable. Therefore, if you build your life upon the stability of God's Word, then, you can better control outcomes, even in dealing with the unpredictability of people's behaviors. The Bible says, "Follow peace with all men, and holiness. Without which no man shall see the Lord" (Hebrews 12:14). It says, "Pursue peace" (Psalm 34:14). It says, "As much as lieth in you live peaceably with all men" (Romans 12:18). The most challenging discipline that we must develop is to take control of our mouth. In the Epistle of James it says, "If a man or woman can control their tongue, they are a perfect person" (according to James 3:2). You can feel many ways in your body, however, if you can control your tongue, then, the Bible says you are a "perfect" or complete and disciplined person. Jesus says, "In your patience possess you your souls" (Luke 21:19). In other words, you keep self-possession of your soul. You keep self-possession of your mind. You keep self-possession of your will. Don't let anyone make you "lose your mind" in anger or fear or in your behavior. "In your patience possess you your soul" (Luke 21:19). In your self-control possess you your soul. In your temperance possess you your soul. Keep self-possessed of your mind, will, emotions, personality, and intellect. If you keep control of your tongue, then, you can most often determine the outcome of the situation. What you say, or don't say, or how you say it, will often determine what comes next in regard to relationships with people. Therefore, this proverb indicates that people respond better to a gentle or "soft answer." Proverbs 15:1 says,

---

1. A soft answer turns away wrath: but grievous words stir up anger.

Even wild animals respond more calmly to soft talking or soft music. Even lions or horses will respond to soft words. Some people are called "horse whisperers." They know how to talk to the animal to calm it down. You have the power to escalate or de-escalate a potentially contentious situation. This is a key to maintaining peace of mind in relationships. Having peace in your relationships is a critical key to "Peace of Mind." Peace of mind is successful living. Having peace of mind improves your health. It lessens the potential of having ulcers in your belly from having so much acid billowing in your stomach from dealing with contentious situations regarding people. Jesus said "Peace I leave with you. My peace give I unto you. Not as the world giveth give I unto you. Let not your heart be troubled. Neither let it be afraid" (John 14:27). He will give us "Peace which passes all understanding" (Philippians 4:7). Philippians 4:4-9 gives us keys to maintaining peace of mind. This will help you "GAIN 20/20 VISION FOR THE NEW DECADE". The keys that we have talked about in this book all work together to help you have "A Step by Step Path To A More Successful Future." We talked about the following keys: 1) God. 2) Marriage & Family. 3) Health. 4) Finances. And, now we're talking about key number 5) Peace of Mind.

The Apostle Paul's Prescription For Peace

The Apostle Paul gives us a "prescription" for peace, that if taken consistently as instructed, we will maintain peace of mind. Philippians 4:9 says, "Rejoice in the Lord alway: and again I say, Rejoice." So, "rejoicing" is a principle that travels from the Old Testament with King David, all the way to the New Testament with the Apostle Paul as a way of maintaining your peace. The Apostle Paul had a lot of trouble and difficulties in his ministry. He was responsible for the various churches that he planted. He also faced the persecution of people trying to kill him. He was stoned, beat, and shipwrecked, etc. Therefore, Apostle Paul had to learn to maintain his internal joy. In the midst of external circumstances, the Apostle Paul had to maintain his internal joy. He had to maintain his internal buoyancy so that his internal soul didn't sink when he was shipwrecked. He had to maintain his internal buoyancy so that he wouldn't sink to the bottom of the sea of life when the billows of life's circumstances began to rage. When the waters of life became rough and it seemed like he would be sunk, then, it wasn't only the plank of wood that held him up and kept him afloat in the dark, cold waters of the sea as it seemed that he was shipwrecked in life. No. It was the internal buoyancy that was brought about from him being filled with God's Word that kept him afloat. He continued to rejoice in the Lord and in the power of His might. Therefore, the Apostle Paul advises us to "Rejoice in the Lord alway: and again I say, Rejoice." He advises us to continue to rejoice in what God said. Now, in Philippians 4:4-9 the Apostle Paul gives us a prescription for how to maintain our peace of mind in the midst of various life situations.

---

4. Rejoice in the Lord alway: and again I say, Rejoice.

5. Let your moderations be known unto all men. The Lord is at hand.

6. Be careful for nothing; but in every thing by prayer and supplication with thanksgiving let your requests be made known unto God.

7. And the peace of God, which passeth all understanding, shall keep your hearts and minds through Christ Jesus.

> 8. Finally, brethren, whatsoever things are true, whatsoever things are honest, whatsoever things are just, whatsoever things are pure, whatsoever things are lovely, whatsoever things are of good report; if there be any virtue, and if there be any praise, think on these things.
>
> 9. Those things, which ye have both learned, and received, and heard, and seen in me, do: and the God of peace shall be with you.

The word "moderation" means "temperance or self-control." It means your ability to regulate your responses in life. It means balance. To be "moderate" means that "you are not too far out to the left and you're not too far out to the right." But, you're balanced. You're not too high. You're not too low. You don't get out of control in anger. You don't get depressed. You are stable. Why? Because, "The Lord is at hand." You know that "God's got this." You walk through life and say, "God's got this." If a situation happens in your life, then, you say, "God's got this."

If you have to deal with a person with a difficult personality, then, you say, "God's got this." If you have to deal with a difficult family situation, then, you say, "God's got this." If a situation of uncertainty arises in the nation, then, you say, "God's got this." Regarding weather threats, you take proper precautions, then, you say, "God's got this." You keep casting your cares upon the Lord, for the Lord cares for you (according to 1 Peter 5:7). "The Lord is at hand." "God's got this." So, you're rejoicing in God's ability. You keep bringing it back up in your mind. You rejoice. You keep giving God the glory. Great is our Lord and greatly to be praised. You're bringing up the greatness of our God. You're rejoicing in His ability to do anything, but fail. You're saying, "I can do all things through Christ, which strengthens me" (Philippians 4:13). You're saying, "If God be for me, then, who can be against me" (Romans 8:31). You're saying, "Greater is He that is in me than he that is in the world" (1 John 4:4). You're saying, "The earth is the Lord's and the fullness thereof. We are His people and the sheep of His pasture" (Psalm 24:1, Psalm 100:3). Rejoice in the Lord! Your "moderation" is self-control. It's your moderateness. Not too high. Not too low. Not too extreme. You have balance. You have peace. Why? Because, "the Lord is at hand." God's got this! The Lord is at hand. He has His hand on the "throttle." In the Hebrew language the Word "hand" here has to do with the word "throttle" like a motorcycle. God controls how much gas gets to your engine of life. He controls how fast things go for you. He controls how much trouble can come. The scripture says, "There is no temptation (or challenge) that has taken you, but such as is common to man; but, God is faithful, who will not suffer you to be tempted above that you are able, but will with the temptation also make a way of escape so that you will be able to bear it" (1 Corinthians 10:13). So, that tells us that if He won't "suffer" it, then, He must be "at hand." He has His hand on whatever your situation or circumstance may be. God says, "I will not allow a situation to happen in your life that's greater than what you're capable of handling, but along with the challenge that comes, I will provide the grace, the answer, or the way of escape so that you're able to bear it. You will be able to bear through it and come through on the other side victoriously. You will be able to make it through that situation." So, you can have peace of mind. Again, Philippians 4:4-9 says,

---

4. Rejoice in the Lord alway: and again I say, Rejoice.

5. Let your moderation be known unto all men. The Lord is at hand.

6. Be careful for nothing; but in every thing by prayer and supplication with thanksgiving let your requests be made known unto God.

7. And the peace of God, which passeth all understanding, shall keep your hearts and minds through Christ Jesus.

8. Finally, brethren, whatsoever things are true, whatsoever things are honest, whatsoever things are just, whatsoever things are pure, whatsoever things are lovely, whatsoever things are of good report; if there be any virtue, and if there be any praise, think on these things.

9. Those things, which ye have both learned, and received, and heard, and seen in me, do: and the God of peace shall be with you.

God is teaching us to maintain our peace and to worry about nothing. God is saying to you "Don't be worried or full of care for nothing." "Nothing" means *nothing*. Zero. Nothing. Be careful for nothing. That includes bills, family, health, weather, situations in the nation, situations in the economy, etc. Be careful for nothing. Don't be full of care for anything. Rather, you should keep casting your care upon the Lord in prayer. He didn't say that you're not concerned about it or aware of it, but you "roll" it over on the Lord. Proverbs 16:3 says, "Commit thy works unto the Lord, and thy thoughts shall be established." "Commit" means to "roll." Roll it over like a *boulder*. That boulder of care that is trying to weigh your heart down, just roll it like you roll a boulder from the top of a hill. You roll it all the way down on the Lord, because He can handle it. You roll that boulder of care off of you down that hill unto the Lord and let it go. Let it go. And, don't you go running after the boulder of care after you let it go. And, if it tries to roll back up the other side of the hill, then, you roll it back down. Every time it comes up, then, you keep casting the care upon the Lord. Keep casting the care. Keep casting the care. And, before you know it, God would've walked you through that situation. And, you will be on the other side of the mountain. Philippians 4:6 says,

> 6. Be careful for nothing; but in every thing by prayer and supplication with thanksgiving let your requests be made known unto God.

God tells us to "be worried about nothing, but in everything by prayer and supplication, with thanksgiving, let your request be made known unto God." That means "in every thing." It means about your job, about your health, about your family, about your neighborhood, about your nation, about your city, about that test that you have to take, about that situation on the job, about your business, etc. You cast your care upon the Lord in prayer. You seek the Lord for his answer with supplication. Then, you give God thanks. You say, "Lord, I thank you that you are able. Thank you for the answer. Thank you Jesus that you have been made unto me wisdom for this situation. I thank you Jesus that by your stripes I was healed, and, therefore, I am healed. Thank you for your grace that is upon me. I can do all things through Christ, which strengthens me. I thank you that greater is He that is in me than he that is in the world. I thank you that if God be for me, then, who can be against me. I give you praise, because You are with me, You are for me, and You're in me." With this type of prayer you're not begging. Rather, you're making your "request" known to the One that is able and willing to help you. You're making a request to the One that you are in relationship with. So, you come before God with your request. Then, in exchange, you get His peace. In this section of the book we are talking about "Peace of Mind." This is a critical key and desire as you "GAIN 20/20 VISION FOR THE NEW DECADE! A Step By Step Path To A More Successful Future." The Apostle Paul didn't say that when you come in prayer, that you will get all of the answers right away, and that you will understand all of the details of what to do right away every time. No. However, you will get this peace, because, you have cast the care of the situation over on the Lord. It didn't say that you wouldn't address the situation, but you are not carrying the load of the situation. You're not carrying the heavy load. You're not burdened down by the situation. Rather, you're trusting God, Who is the source of all wisdom. You're trusting God, Who is the source of all strength. You're trusting God, Who is the source of all ability. You're trusting God, Who is the source of all knowledge, wisdom, and insight into every situation and circumstance. God sees the heart of every person. He sees it. He's there. He can. He cares. You are casting your care upon Him. So, you're not carrying that heavy load, because you're in relationship with the One that can do it! You don't have to wait until your understanding catches up for you to have the peace. Rather, God's peace passes understanding. God's peace will "guard" your heart. He will "keep your heart and mind." He will keep your internal heart. He will keep you from internal stress and turmoil. This will also protect your health. He will keep you from being full of anxiety in your heart. He will keep you from ulcers. He will keep you from acid indigestion and your food not digesting right. He will keep you from having internal turmoil. He will keep or guard your heart. God will guard your "heart and mind." Your mind won't be confused and mixed up. You won't be full of perplexity. Rather, you will have peace, because God is guarding your heart and your mind by Christ Jesus. Philippians 4: 8 goes on to say,

---

> 8. Finally, brethren, whatsoever things are true, whatsoever things are honest, whatsoever things are just, whatsoever things are pure, whatsoever things are lovely, whatsoever things are of good report; if there be any virtue, and if there be any praise, think on these things.

The Apostle Paul tells you how to maintain this "Peace of Mind". He uses the word "whatsoever". The word "whatsoever" is a very comprehensive word. You have a lot of choices of things to think. Think on things that are "true", "honest", "just", "pure", "lovely", and of "good report." It can be something as natural as "My team won the game this Sunday." That's a "good report" if you enjoy sports. God wants you to have some relaxation. That's a good report, rather than, just thinking about your problems. You will still address the responsibilities of life, but, if you can take a moment to say a "Horrah!" with your team, then, that's a good report. Or, you may have gotten a letter from a friend or a phone call that tells you that they're doing well or a family member that tells you they're doing well, then, that's a "good report." Philippians 4:9 continues by saying,

9. Those things, which ye have both learned, and received, and heard, and seen in me, do: and the God of peace shall be with you.

As a result of following the Apostle Paul's prescription, then, the resulting end will be peace. He says, "The God of peace shall be with you." This is a critical key to "Peace of Mind." "Peace of Mind" is critical for you to "GAIN 20/20 VISION FOR THE NEW DECADE! A Step By Step Path To A More Successful Future."

The Key To Happiness

In most cases, peace is the key to happiness. Maintaining peace often comes down to living peaceable with others. Proverbs 20:3 says, "It is an honor for a man to cease from strife: but every fool will be meddling." In other words, it is an honorable thing for you to cease from saying or doing things that will cause strife in your relationships, business dealings, family life, etc. It's honorable when you develop enough self-control that you choose peace, rather than fighting for your right to be right. The Bible says that it's "foolish" to continue to say things or do things that stir up trouble. You must pursue peace in your relationships, in your financial life, in your health, etc. If you know that what you are about to do or say will cause trouble, then, don't do it or say it. Rather, choose peace. If it's not necessary that you say it or do it, then, don't. However, there are some things that you just have to address in life and let the *"chips fall where they may."* Sometimes you have to confront a situation. If you don't confront it, then, the situation won't change for the better. Nevertheless, you can do it in an honorable, confident way without being argumentative. You can address it courageously so that you resolve the problem. Therefore, you're seeking peace, because you are seeking to solve the problem. Addressing and solving the issue is always better than allowing the problems to continue, due to your fear of facing it. Often, through confronting problems, then, greater peace is ultimately obtained. You can't just let a situation *ride*. Most situations won't go away on it's own. Rather, it has to be dealt with. Yet, you want to address the problem in the most peaceable manner possible. Ultimately, you're seeking peace. Proverbs 3:13–18 says:

> 13. Happy is the man that finds wisdom, and the man that gets understanding.

14. For the merchandise of it is better than the merchandise of silver, and the gain thereof than fine gold.

15. She is more precious than rubies: and all the things thou can desire are not to be compared unto her.

16. Length of days is in her right hand; and in her left hand riches and honor.

17. Her ways are ways of pleasantness, and all her paths are peace.

18. She is a tree of life to them that lay hold upon her: and happy is everyone that retains her.

As we have explored these keys to help you "GAIN 20/20 VISION FOR THE NEW DECADE! A Step By Step Path To More Successful Future", we have come down to the bottom line of what we all want.

We all want to be *happy*. We all want an enjoyable life. We all want to be healthy. We're all seeking a better relationship with God our Creator. We all should desire a healthy marriage and family life. We all want financial prosperity and success. And, ultimately we all want peace. The Bible says in Proverbs 3:13 "Happy is the man that finds wisdom, and the man that gets understanding." The Bible promises the person who finds God's wisdom will obtain happiness. Proverbs 3:14 continues, "For the merchandise of it is better than the merchandise of silver, and the gain thereof than fine gold." God promises that those who obtain His wisdom are obtaining "merchandise" that is more valuable than silver and gold. You are obtaining tangible substance from your relationship with God. The Bible tells us that we should "cry out for wisdom", and "search for wisdom as for precious silver." We should seek it out by walking with God day by day. In Proverbs 3:15 it says, "She is more precious than rubies: and all the things you can desire or not to be compared unto her." God's wisdom is the most important and most precious thing we could have in life. God's wisdom comes from the Holy Spirit. We obtain relationship with the Holy Spirit through our relationship with Jesus Christ as Lord and Savior. The Bible says, "Whosoever shall call upon the name of the Lord shall be saved" (Romans 10:13). That is the key to our salvation. Calling on the name of Jesus is the key to a bright future in this world and into eternity. If you've never received Jesus Christ as Lord and Savior, then, that is the beginning of wisdom for you. Wisdom from God starts with relationship with God. It starts with recognizing that you need God. Whoever calls out to God for salvation will be saved. Accepting Jesus Christ as Lord and Savior is the beginning of wisdom. The Bible promises that truly walking in relationship with Jesus Christ as Lord and Savior, and obtaining God's wisdom on a continual basis, will extend your life on this Earth. God will lead you to obtain "riches and honor" (Proverbs 3:16). God also promises He will give you peace. Finally, Proverbs 3:18 says, "She is a tree of life to them that lay hold upon her: and happy is everyone that retains her." Jesus Christ is the source of wisdom and happiness for us today. God sent his Son into the world to deliver us from sin, sickness, disease, poverty, failed relationships, and alienation from God. Our relationship is restored through our faith in what Jesus did for us through His death, burial, and resurrection. Clarity of vision starts with your relationship with God, your Creator and Heavenly Father, through accepting the free gift of salvation offered by the sacrifice of His holy Son Jesus Christ. Jesus died on the cross to pay for your sins and God, the Father, raised Him from the dead for your salvation. Your sin debt is paid-in-full through the death, burial, and resurrection of Jesus Christ. John 3:16–17 says,

---

16. For God so loved the world, that he gave his only begotten Son, that whosoever believes in him should not perish, but have everlasting life.

17. For God sent not his Son into the world to condemn the world; but that the world through him might be saved.

If you've never received Jesus Christ as Lord and Savior, I would like you to pray this prayer right now in faith. Ask Him to come into your heart, and be your Lord and Savior. Simply say this:

"Jesus, I believe you are the Son of God. I believe you died on the cross to pay for my sins. I accept your payment for my sins. I believe God raised you from the dead for my salvation. I accept salvation. I accept you as my Lord and Savior. I will live the rest of my life for you. Thank you Lord Jesus for being my Savior. Thank you. I will spend eternity in Heaven with you and the Heavenly Father when my life on Earth over. In Your name, Jesus, I pray, Amen."

Final Words

These are the foundational keys to help you "GAIN 20/20 VISION FOR THE NEW DECADE! A STEP BY STEP PATH TO A MORE SUCCESSFUL FUTURE." If you have gained clarity regarding this truth, then, you have gained the clear focus that you need in order to have a successful new decade, future, and eternity. These are the keys to gaining success in life and in your future through your relationship with 1) God. 2) Marriage & Family. 3) Health. 4) Finances. 5) Peace of Mind. For more keys to successful living please get a copy of my book series Distinguished Wisdom Presents... "Living Proverbs": Over 530 New Wisdom Insights For Contemporary Times. The series currently contains Distinguished Wisdom Presents... "Living Proverbs"-Vol.1, Vol. 2, Vol.3, Vol.4, and Vol.5. Distinguished Wisdom Presents... "Living Proverbs"-Vol.6 will coming soon. The book series is full of daily guidance and insight to help you make better and faster godly decisions. It will help you navigate the new dynamics of the new decade and future. Be encouraged as you go forward into your future. God's principles are reliable in any environment. No matter what changes or storms may arise upon the unpredictable ocean of life ahead, you will now be able to safely navigate your life through the clear vision gained from God's wisdom. You will be able to overcome, stand, and be victorious in life! Please share this book with your family and friends as a guide for their future. Also, please be sure to write your reviews and recommendations for this book on the websites that you purchased it from in order to suggest it to others who can be blessed by this resource of guidance and comfort. Thank you.

My prayer for you in the new decade is: "May your life be enriched by the words of wisdom!" God bless you

ABOUT THE AUTHOR

Pastor Terrance Levise Turner, MBA is the founder and president of Well Spoken Inc., a media company in Nashville, TN. He is a graduate of Tennessee State University, with a MBA in Finance & Supply

Chain Management and a Bachelor of Speech Communication and Theater (Mass Media) from the same university. He is the author of several books, including the Distinguished Wisdom Presents . . . *"Living Proverbs"* series, Distinguished Wisdom Presents . . . *Your Wealth Is In Your Anointing: Discover Keys To Releasing Your Potential*, Distinguished Wisdom Presents . . . *The Dynamic Victory Confession: Powerful Confessions For A Victorious Life*, and a children's book titled *"The Earth Is Sad, Little Timmy"*. His books are available at www.TerranceTurnerLivingProverbs.com. He is an accomplished singer/songwriter/recording artist. He and his wife, Avis, sing and minister together. His books and music is available on all your favorite sites. Pastor Turner and his wife Avis live in Nashville, TN.

www.ingramcontent.com/pod-product-compliance
Lightning Source LLC
Chambersburg PA
CBHW021059080526
44587CB00010B/302